Kick Start Automation Testing

Irrespective of programming knowledge

Learn Selenium with Java

Amol Ujagare

DEDICATION

This book is dedicated to my late grandparents
(Chandrakant Ujagare, Shalini Ujagare)

CONTENTS

ACKNOWLEDGMENTS

As you have got this book, you must be someone who has at least awareness of software testing or you might have worked in manual testing for a couple of years. Initially, we chose this career option because we wanted to go into the IT industry and we also never wanted to learn to program so we thought that software testing is the best. Later on, we realized that just the knowledge of software testing (manual) is not enough. To grow, we must also know automation. But to learn automation, we must also learn programming. Now, this is the big challenge. To overcome this challenge let me be the captain of your ship. I have come up with this book which will not only help you to overcome your programming fear but will also give you a little more confidence to implement the automation as well.

To make the best use of this book please implement your learning on your own machine. Because this is a real-time industry where just the awareness of certain technology is not enough you must be able to implement it as well.

So all the very best to start your journey.

ABOUT THE AUTHOR

Hello, I completed my Engineering in information technology from PICT (Pune Institute of computer technology), and I worked in the software industry for more than 7 years.

I initially started my career as a java developer. Later on, I moved to Software testing. Manual testing might help you to start your career in the IT industry but you must learn automation to achieve excellence in your career. Well, I learned and implemented automation in my organization. Here I got to learn many things from scratch. It was a small organization. You might have heard that you get to learn a lot in a small organization. I actually experienced it.

Since when I started my Academics till now, I experienced lots of challenges and failures. Today when I look back, I feel that the best things that happened to me are my failures. Because of those only I learned to get up and walk. Once our HOD said in some ceremony that there is one difference between school/college learning and learning lessons from life.

"In school/college you first learn the lesson then there is an exam, but in life first there is an exam then you learn the lesson."

Section – 1

The Java Programming

1.1   JAVA INTRODUCTION

Introduction to programming:
We will enter the automation testing world with selenium. We can implement selenium in a few different languages; Java is one. So, we need to learn Java.

Java is a programming language. Let's understand more about programming.

Programming needs: If we are planning to move to automation testing, then the programming knowledge is not that deeper is essential. Because in automation, we need to use some readily available functions (created by someone) that will help us automate the various scenarios.

Program & code:
what is a program? A program is nothing but a set of instructions.
If I ask you the difference between programming & coding, are they the same or different? Of course, they are different
suppose you want to wash the clothes with a washing machine, you put all the clothes inside it then, you press some buttons, you set the water level you set the mode & then you start the machine, can I say that you programmed the washing machine? Yes, because you set some instructions
Another example: suppose you want to cook food in an oven, you put the bowl of vegetables inside it, then you set its mode, you set temperature, you set time & start, can I say that you programmed the oven? Yes, because you put some instructions.

Setting or giving the instructions to a particular machine is programming, the mechanism that makes everything happen is code. So yes, code is something that makes it happen the things you instructed.

Java Programming:
Now, we can do coding in different languages like C, C++, and Java. When I say Language, consider a language that you speak; you might have learned its grammar, more or less, isn't it? If we know the grammar of a language, then working with the language means either speaking or writing may be reading also will not be a big deal.

So, let's understand the grammar of the Java language. You may see the word 'syntax' somewhere around; if you are new to this word, then please don't be surprised. It is nothing but the way we write the code (statements in the program)

Grammar means a set of rules. And consider the below rules.
1. every program has a starting point, and in most programming languages, it is the 'main' function - we start with

Generally, in c or c++, it is,
void main()

1. in Java, the 'main' function is written as follows

```
public static void main (String[] args)
{

}
```

we use opening & closing curly brackets to specify the start and end of the 'main' function

2. specifically for Java, the 'main' function is inside the class. For example,

```
class NameOfClass
{
```

```
public static void main(String[] args)
{

}


}
```

the outer opening & closing curly brackets around the 'main' function [public static void main(String[] args)] are to specify the start and end of the class

Note: in the syntax, only the 'S' of String is capital rest all are small (apart from 'NameOfClass' - because it is variable, it can be anything given by the programmer)

Now you must be surprised with so many new words here as below
class
public
static
void
String
args

Don't worry; we have proper complete chapters to understand this right now. Just consider this format as it is, & now we will write the first java program.
First Java program, compile & run.
Before we start talking more about the programming, I want you should have the below softwares installed on your machines
a. java
b. intellij idea
c. eclipse
Just search on Google & download its setup based on your operating system. and install it. Installing it is again not rocket science; open the setup & keep all the default settings; keep on saying next --> & it will get installed (all three)
only while installing the eclipse, you might see several options at the beginning like eclipse for java developer, etc. choose the first one that is "eclipse for java developer. " The first option is shown below.

First Java Program

Let's start with a first java program - print hello world

as we have seen the format/structure of the java program above, I would like to tell you that please consider the below conventions while giving names to the class and variables

1. Always use some meaningful words for the class name or for variables to make your code readable & user-friendly.
2. The class name should start with a capital letter & use a camel case
3. variable name should begin with a small letter & use a camel case

Now, what is a camel case? The Camel case is nothing but forming a text with different words used; here, the first letter of the next word is capital. Below are some examples of the words in the camel case
a. HelloWorld
b. MyClass
c. addVariables
d. rightAngle
so, let's switch to the printing of "hello world" to print anything by the program below is the command in Java
System. out.println("Text to be printed");
[there is a semicolon after completion of each statement]
so, consider the below program

```
class HelloWorld
{
        public static void main(String[] args)
        {
                System.out.println("Hello World");
        }
}
```

In this way, you will write a program to print 'hello world.' Now the question is where to write it.
you can write it in notepad/eclipse or Intellij Idea
the eclipse & IntelliJ idea we will discuss in the next chapter right now let's write in notepad

HelloWord.java - Notepad

File Edit Format View Help

```
class HelloWorld
{

public static void main(String[] args)
{
   System.out.println("Hello World");
}


}
```

Now save this file with the same name as a class name at some location. Say if you are using windows on 'D' drive, I am creating a folder as 'MyProg.' To run this program or execute the thing we have written.

Remember that there are two steps for running or executing a program

1. compile

2. Run

Now, if you are writing a java program in notepad, you have to do these steps on the command prompt, so open the command prompt (if you have Linux max, then open terminal) and reach the folder where you have kept the java file.

Now to reach that particular folder, follow the below steps

1. type drive name followed by a colon ':', then enter

2. type cd followed by the path of the folder

Now you are at the particular folder; we can now hit the commands, compile & run.

A. Compile: to compile, the command is as below

javac filename.java

B. Run: to run, below is the command

java className

if your program does not have any errors, it will run. Otherwise, you have to fix those errors and then again compile and run, so here the program is

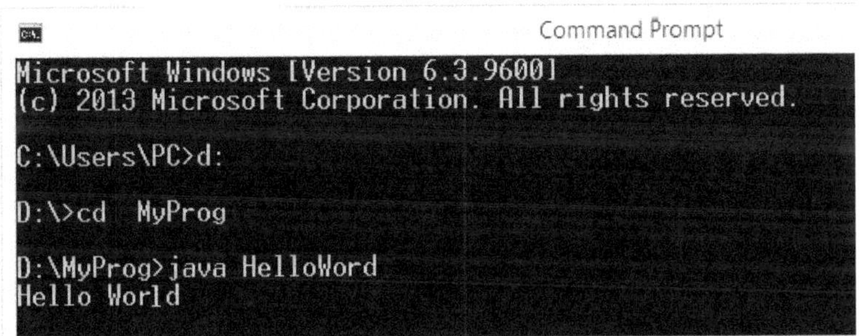

the class name is Hello world, So we have saved it as HelloWorld.java

1. Compile: javac HelloWord.java

2. Run: java HelloWorld

output will be

1.2 JAVA BASICS

In the last chapter, we have seen the basic structure of a java program. And how to compile and run the program. In this chapter, we will try to do some more programs. But we should have some more understanding of programming, so here I will introduce some variables.

Suppose I want to represent an integer number, and I want to create a variable. I will create as below

int a;

you can store the value in it like

a =10;

or you may also write like int a =10;

if you want to represent a decimal value, you can create a variable in 2 ways

1. float : float f = 77.13;
2. double : double d = 23.46;

you can also store a single character (e.g., a, f, #,@, etc.) into a variable of type char, e.g., char c ='g' ; (we have to use a single quote around the character)

boolean is also a type wherein you can store true or false like a values
And there are some more but right now, understand these. we will use these first and slowly, step by step, we need the others. I will introduce you to that as well.

let's do the following program

Take two variables a & b, put some values to them, do the Addition, and print it.

consider below program

```
class Addition
{

public static void main(String[] args)
{

  int  a = 10 ;
  int  b = 20 ;
  int  c;

  c = a + b;

System.out.println(c);

}

}
```

As per requirement, a & b are the two integer variables in the above program. We have assigned them values. We are doing the Addition on the next line, and then we are printing it. While printing, you must have observed that I have put 'c' in System.out.println(), which means you can set the variable in it & get it printed. But make sure that you should not write variables with double-quotes.

```
D:\MyProg>java Addition
30
```

Above is the output after running

you can make a small change in the last line as below

System.out.println("Addition=" + c);

And the output will be as below

```
D:\MyProg>java Addition
Addition=30
```

Yes, you can attach a text with the variable value. It's just that text you have to write in double quote & variable without the double quote. and to concatenate, use the plus(+) symbol

Based on this, below are some assignments for you
1. take two numbers and do subtraction, multiplication, division operation
2. take two decimal numbers and do Addition, subtraction, multiplication, the division operation

Operators in Java
Before we jump into the different java topics, one essential thing you need to know is operators in java.
There are two types of operators
1. Binary operators
2. Unary operators
1. Binary operators: as the name suggests, these operators operate on two operands. for example
a + b
a - b (here a & b are operands)
A few more binary operators are as below
< , > , <= ,>=
We use these operators to compare two similar types of variables or variables with value.
for example.
a > b , a >= b , a < 10 , a <= 10
Here any of the above statements will either return a true or false value, which will be in the Boolean format.

1.3 CONTROL STRUCTURE

Suppose you want to bring a grocery by your mother one day. And you have two options for the shop, one shop is near to you, and one shop is 5 to 10 min farther. If it is a Wednesday, then in the second shop, you get 20 % off. While on other days, it's a regular price. In the first shop, there is no such offer.

Now, if I ask you which shop you will go to? The answer is simple it depends. If it is Wednesday, you will surely go to the second shop where there is a discount.

So, consider the below diagram.

Shop 1 - No discount
Shop 2 - Discount on wednesday

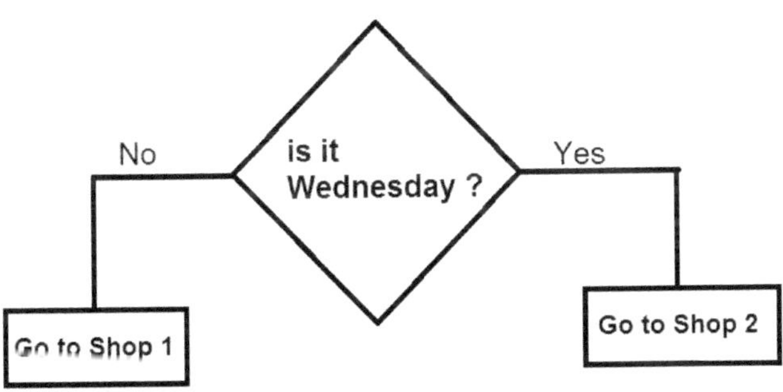

Let's take one more example, suppose there are two integer variables with values 10 & 20, respectively, as below,

int a =10;

int b=20;

print which one is greater, for that consider below flow chart

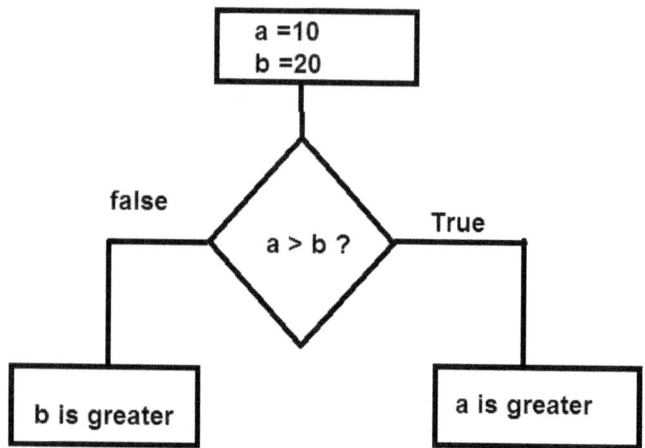

The same can be implemented in programming as well using if-else.
Below is the syntax (the way of writing the code)
Syntax :
if(condition)
{
    statements;
}
else
{
    statements;
}

In front of it, We must mention the condition. If the condition is true, then the program execution control will go into if block & statements inside this if block will run. If the condition is not true, the control will come to the 'else' part, and the statements inside the 'else' parts will run.
for example
int a =10;
int b =20;
if(a>b)

```
{
System.out.println("a is greater");
}
else
{
System.out.println("b is greater")
}
```

try this program in IntelliJ Idea or eclipse and verify the output

Let's see one more example :

consider, int marks= 57; let this be out of 100, based on the value of the marks state is it pass, fail, first-class, second class or Distinction

we know that

if marks < 40, then it will be failed

1. if marks >= 40 and marks <50 then it pass
2. if marks >= 50 and marks <60, then it will be second class
3. if marks >= 60 and marks <75then it will be first class
4. if marks >= 75, then it will be a Distinction

We can code the same as below.

```java
1   public class Marks {
2
3       public static void main(String[] args) {
4
5           int marks = 50;
6
7           if(marks<40)
8               System.out.println("fail");
9
10          else if(marks >=40 && marks < 50)
11              System.out.println("pass");
12
13          else if (marks >= 50 && marks <60)
14              System.out.println("second class");
15
16          else if (marks >=60 && marks < 75)
17              System.out.println("First class");
18
19          else if(marks > 75)
20              System.out.println("Distinction");
21      }
22  }
```

Let's do one more program. Do you know the types of triangles? I am sure you know. Consider the below diagram.

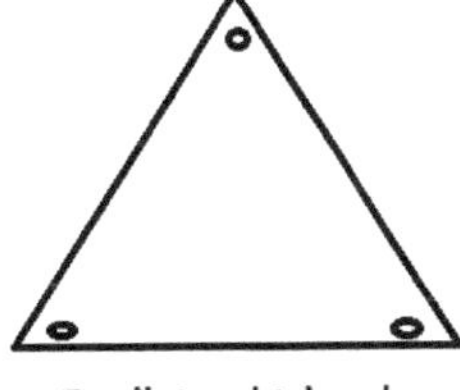

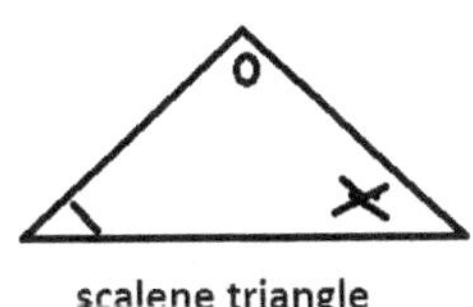

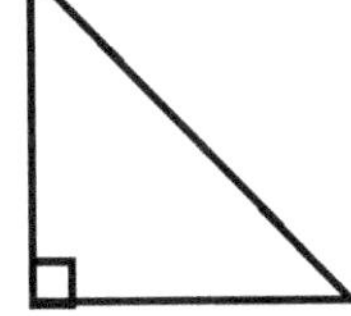

Types of triangle:-

consider 3 integer variables

a =

b=

c=

let's put some value to it

a = 30

b= 70

c= 80

Based on the values, state what type of Triangle it is

Now we know how the triangles are, as you can see in the diagram as well.

case 1: equilateral Triangle

all the angles are equal

a==b && b ==c && c ==a

Now here, I have used two operators,

a.' ==': This operator compares two things (variable with variable or variable with the number). It gives a result in Boolean, either true or false

b. '&&': This operator is called an AND operator. It combines two conditions & gives the result.
For example: consider a is one condition and b is another condition. Below is the table, that explains the result of the AND operator on the conditions. a & b

a	b	a && b
True	False	False
False	True	False
False	False	False
True	True	True

so let's come back to case 1
we have to check whether a, b, and c are equal or not
we can check
'a' should be equal to 'b' and 'b' should be equal to 'c' that's it, because if 'a' and 'b' are equal then it ultimately means that 'a' and 'c' are equal'
so the condition would be
if(a==b && b==c)
System.out.println("Equilateral triangle");

case 2: scalene triangle :
!= we will use this operator for not equal to check
here the condition will be
if(a!=b && b!=c)
System.out.println("Scalene triangle ");

case 3: Right-angled Triangle
here we are supposed to check whether either of the angles is 90 degrees or not.
we will check this with or operator (||) Just like an operator, but it works in a different way
a==90 || b==90 || c==90
here or operator works as below
below is the table that explains the result of the or operator on the conditions a & b

a	b	a || b
True	True	True
True	False	True
False	True	True
False	False	False

case 4: Isosceles Triangle
In this type of a triangle, two angles are equal, and the third one will not be equal
so can I do it as below
a==b && b! =c
Well, this won't be sufficient. Here, we assume that 'a' & 'b' are equal, but 'b' & 'c' could also be equal or 'c' & 'a' could be equal. see the diagram below.

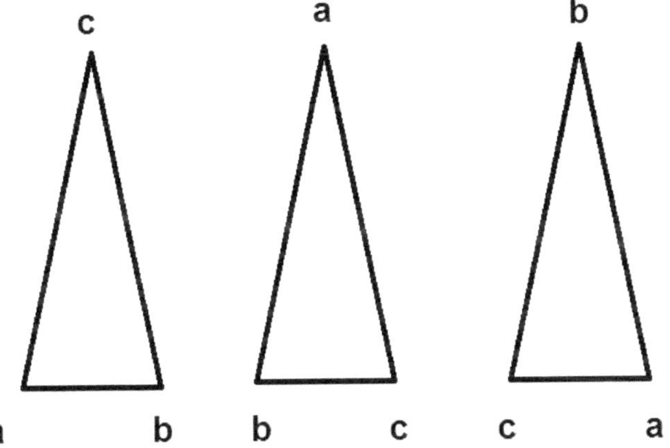

so, we need to write a condition that should work for all of them

so, it would be as below

if((a==b&&b!=c) || (b==c && c!=a) || (c==a && a!=b))

System.out.println("Isosceles Triangle");

so the final code is as below

```
public class Triangle {

    public static void main(String[] args) {

        int a = 30;
        int b = 60;
        int c = 90;

        if (a == b && b == c)
            System.out.println("Equilateral triangle");

         if (a != b && b != c)
            System.out.println("Scalene triangle");

        if (a == 90 || b == 90 || c == 90)
            System.out.println("Right angled triangle");

         if ((a == b && b != c) || (b == c && c != a) || (c == a && a != b))
            System.out.println("Isosceles triangle");

        }
    }
}
```

Now the addition of all angles of a triangle is always 180

none of the angles can't be either zero or negative. so let's add these conditions also to the program

```
public class Triangle {

    public static void main(String[] args) {

        int a = 30;
        int b = 60;
        int c = 90;

        if(a+b+c==180 && a > 0 && b> 0 && c >0)
        {
            if (a == b && b == c)
                System.out.println("Equilateral triangle");

             if (a != b && b != c)
                System.out.println("Scalene triangle");

            if (a == 90 || b == 90 || c == 90)
                System.out.println("Right angled triangle");

             if ((a == b && b != c) || (b == c && c != a) || (c == a && a != b))
                System.out.println("Isosceles triangle");

        }
        else
            System.out.println("This is a not a triangle");

        }
    }
}
```

So we have seen three different types of examples of if-else
1. simple if-else, wherein we had just a single if and single else
2. if-else if ladder (marks example). When we find the condition is true, the control of a program stops execution, and no further conditions get checked
3. multiple if (Triangle) here, every condition gets checked.

Switch Case:
We go for a switch case when you have multiple cases to be checked and want the control to jump to the corresponding case and execute it directly.
consider the below example
The syntax of the switch case is as below
switch(option)
{

       case option1 : statements ; break;
       case option2 : statements ; break;
       case option2 : statements ; break;

       -

       -

       case option-n : statements ; break;
default : System.out.println("wrong choice"); break
}
It means we get a choice/option, and based on that, we directly jump to the particular case, and if your choice/option does not match any case, then default statements will run.
Note: A' break' is written in every case (even in default). When your statements inside the case execute, the control should come out of the switch case. Now consider the below example.

```java
public class SwitchDemo {

    public static void main(String[] args) {

        int a = 10;
        int b =5;
        int c;

        String operation = "add";

        switch (operation)
        {

            case "add" : c = a + b ;
                System.out.println("Addition="+c);
                break;

            case "substract" : c = a - b;
                System.out.println("Substraction="+c);
                break;

            case "mulitplication" : c = a * b;
                System.out.println("Multiplication="+c);
                break;

            case "division" : c = a/b;
                System.out.println("Division="+c);
                break;

            default:
                System.out.println("wrong choice");
                break;
        }
    }
}
```

1.4 LOOPS

One fine day my wife told me to get a particular brand of oats from a grocery store. It was not there, and actually, no other store keeps that brand. The shopkeeper said that it might be available tomorrow or 2-3 days. So, it became my daily routine to go to that shop and ask for the oats. one day, I finally got it, and then I stopped going to the shop to buy the oats.

so Actually, I was in a loop until the condition became true

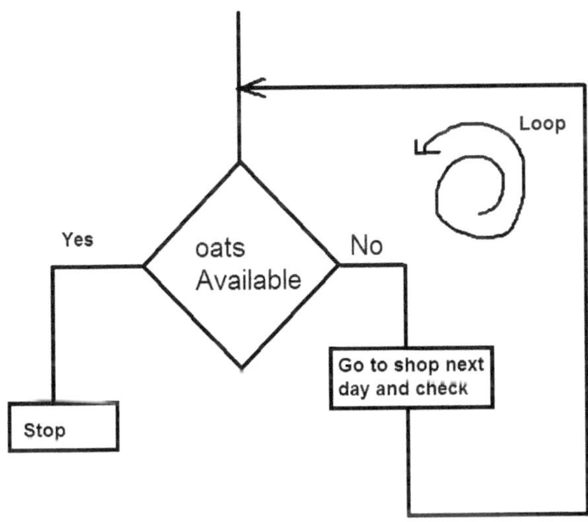

The while loop is the same

below is the syntax

while(condition)

{

        statements;

}

although it looks like if-else, there is a difference as below

if(condition)

{

        statements;

}

Here in the above syntax, if the condition is true, then the statements are executed & if it is false, the control won't go to the if block. In both cases, control comes out of the if block.

but in the while loop, if the condition is false again, the control goes back & it keeps on checking whether the condition is true or not; consider the below flow chart

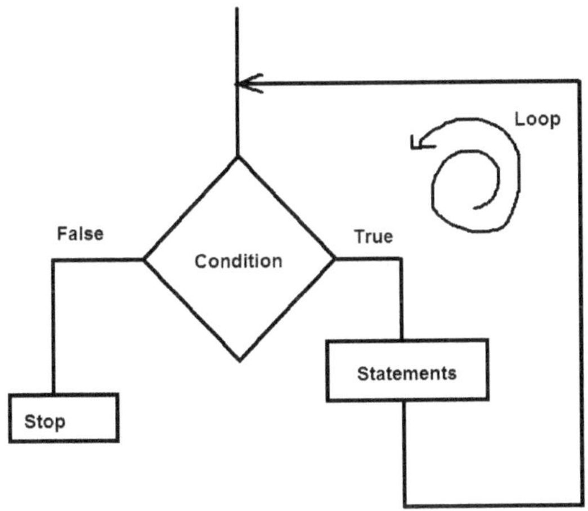

for example, print 1 to 10 numbers

below is the program for that.

```java
public class WhileDemo {

    public static void main(String[] args) {

        int i = 1; // initialization

        while(i<=10) // condition checking
        {
            System.out.println(i);
            i=i++; // increment
        }

    }
}
```

Let's see how this is getting executed
initially, the value of 'i' is one, so we check it in the while loop.
Whether 'i' is less than 10 or not. If yes, the control will go inside the
loop; it will print the value of 'i' & The 'i' will be incremented by 1

(i= i+1). Now the control will go back, and it will check again if the value of 'i' is less than 10, again yes, because now it is 2, this will continue till the value of 'i' becomes 11, now 11 is greater than 10, so the condition will become false. The control will come out of the loop. So in the way, 1 to 10 numbers will be printed.

Do while loop :
the do-while loop also works just like the while loop, and it has just one different thing
in the do-while loop, once the statements are executed without checking the condition (in 'while loop,' first the condition is checked, then the statements are executed)
Below is the syntax

do

{

       Statements;

} while(condition);

Below is the flow chart of do while loop.

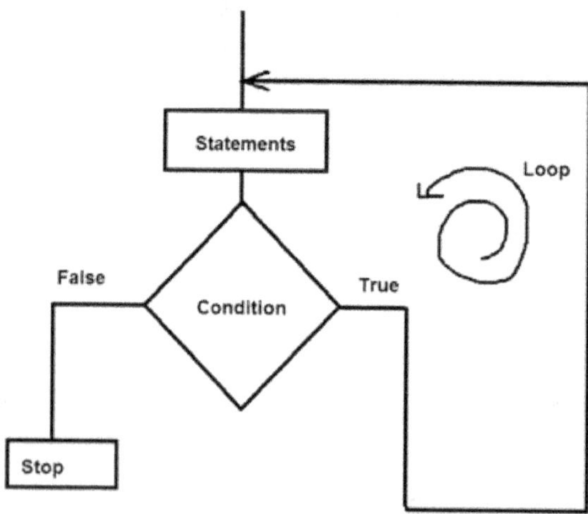

Let's see the same program of printing 1 to 10 numbers using 'while loop.'

```java
public class DoWhileDemo {
    public static void main(String[] args) {
        int i = 1;
        do {
            System.out.println(i);
            i=i+1;

        }while (i<=10);
    }
}
```

For loop:
Always remember that there are three things involved in all the loops
(while, do-while, for)
1. initialization
2. condition checking
3. increment or decrement
the syntax for the 'for' loop is as below

for(initialization ; condition checking ; inc/dec)

{

statements;

}

if you want to print 1 to 10 numbers, below is the code

```java
public class ForloopDemo {

    public static void main(String[] args) {

        for(int i=1;i<=10;i++) {
                System.out.println(i);
        }
    }
}
```

Another example, if you want to print 10 to 1 number, below is the code.

```java
public class ForloopDemo {

    public static void main(String[] args) {

        for(int i=10;i>=1;i--) {
                System.out.println(i);
        }
}
}
```

In above 2 examples you might have observed while doing increment of decrement, we have used i++ , i--

earlier we did this using i=i+1 or i =i-1 this way

so what is this i++ or i--

actually ++ & -- are unary operators they can be used before or after the variable

a. After variable

i++ / i-- : it first executes the statement & then increments / decrements

b. Before variable

++i / -- i : it first increments / decrements & executes the statement

to understand this, consider the below program


```java
public class IncDecDemo {

    public static void main(String[] args) {

        int i = 10;
```

```
    System.out.println(i);
        System.out.println(i++);
        System.out.println(i);
    System.out.println(++i);
        System.out.println(i);
        }
}
```

out put :

10

10

11

12

12

there is a total of five statements printed. Let's understand each, one by one.

1. **i** - here, the value of i is printed as it is that is 10
2. **i++** - as we discussed, i++ will execute the statement first, and then the increment will happen so that it will execute the statement, and we saw that it prints 10
3. **i** - here, the increment that happened in the last statement is now reflected, and 11 is printed
4. **++i** - here, the first increment happens, and then the statement is executed, so incremented value 12 is printed
5. **i** - the current value of i, that is 12, is printed here

let's see another program


```
public class IncDecDemo {

    public static void main(String[] args) {

        int i = 10;

            System.out.println(i);
            System.out.println(i--);
            System.out.println(i);
```

```java
            System.out.println(--i);
            System.out.println(i);


        }

    }
}
```

output :

10
10
9
8
8

there is a total of five statements printed. Let's understand each, one by one.

1. **i** - here, the value of i is printed as it is that is 10
2. **i--** - as we discussed, i-- will execute the statement first, and then the decrement will happen, so the statement executed, and we saw that it prints 10
3. **i** - here, the decrement in the last statement is now reflected, and it prints 9.
4. **--i** - here, the first decrement happens, and then the statements are executed, so incremented value 8 is printed
5. **i** - the current value of i, that is 8, is printed here

Below are some more examples based on for loop
1. even odd problem: write a program to print 1 to 10 numbers and also print odd or even in front of it

Below is the program

```java
public class EvenOddDemo {

    public static void main(String[] args) {

        for (int i = 1; i <= 10; i++) {

            if (i%2 == 0)

                System.out.println(i+" Even");

            else
```

```java
            System.out.println(i+" Odd");

        }

     }

  }
```

Fizz buzz problem: write a program to print 1 to 10 numbers.
1. If the number is divisible by 3 → print → no. Fizz
2. If the number is divisible by 5 → print → no. Buzz
3. If the number is divisible by 3 & 5 → Print → no. FizzBuzz
4. If the number is not divisible by 3 or 5 →
Print → no.
Below is the program


```java
public class FizzBuzz {

  public static void main(String[] args) {

    for(int i=1; i<=30 ;i++)  {

      if(i%3==0 && i%5==0)

        System.out.println(i+" FizzBuzz");

      else if(i%3==0)

        System.out.println(i+" Fizz");

      else if(i%5 == 0)

        System.out.println(i+" Buzz");

      else

        System.out.println(i);

    }

  }
```

}

factorial of a number: Given int n = 5; print the factorial of 5 (5!)

now 5! means

5! = 5 x 4 x 3 x 2 x1

consider the Program below

```java
public class FactorialDemo {
   public static void main(String[] args) {
      int n = 6;
      int mult = 1 ;
      for (int i = n; i >= 1; i--) {
         mult = mult * i ;
      }
      System.out.println("Factorial="+mult);
   }
}
```

the logic behind it is that there are a total of 5 iterations & those are explained below

initially n = 5 , mult = 1 , i = 5

1. mult = 1 , i = 5

mult = mult x i ;
      = 1 x 5 ;
      = 5;

2. mult = 5 , i = 4

mult = mult * i ;
      = 1 x 5 x 4;
      = 5 x 4;

3. mult = 5 x 4 , i = 3
mult = mult * i ;

  = 5 x 4 x 3;

4. mult = 5 x 4 x 3 , i = 2
mult = mult * i ;
  = 5 x 4 x 3 x 2;

5. mult = 5 x 4 x 3 x 2 , i = 1
mult = mult * i ;
  = 5 x 4 x 3 x 2 x 1;

4. Fibonacci series :Given n = 6; print the n numbers of the fibonacci series
What is a Fibonacci series ??
Some numbers in fibonacci series
0 1 1 2 3 5 8 13 21 34 …..

Consider the above series of a number in that the first two terms will come directly, and actually, the Fibonacci series says that two terms are added. The result of the addition creates the next. We also arc willing to do the same we are supposed to generate the series based on how many numbers we want to print in the series. Hence, we must consider the following logic
let's take a and b as two variables, let a =0 and b=1. We will take one more variable, sum =0, and let's take another variable, n = 6, which means we are supposed to print the 6 numbers in the series. So initially, we know that a is =0 and b=1 now, the sum will be a + b, and this will be my third term; now b will become a, and the sum will become b; again, we will add a with b and sum will be a + b. and so on it will be continued until we reached to the 6, Refer below diagram of logic and code is also there

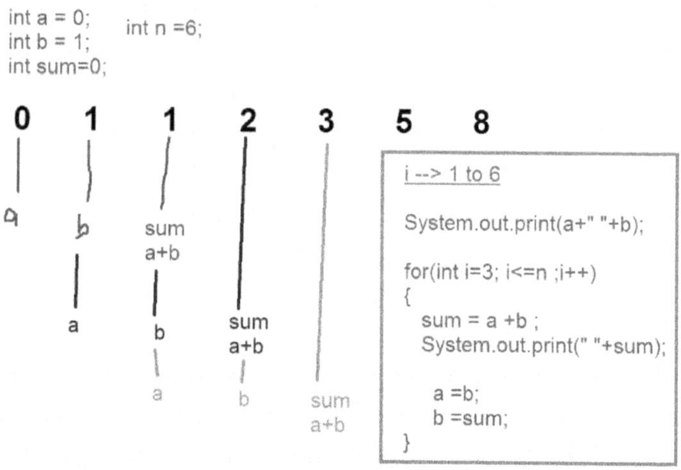

```
int a = 0;      int n =6;
int b = 1;
int sum=0;
```

0   1   1   2   3   5   8

a

b
a

sum
a+b
b
a

sum
a+b
b

sum
a+b

```
i --> 1 to 6

System.out.print(a+" "+b);

for(int i=3; i<=n ;i++)
{
  sum = a +b ;
  System.out.print(" "+sum);

  a =b;
  b =sum;
}
```

```java
public class FibonancciDemo {
  public static void main(String[] args) {

    int a =0 ;
    int b =1 ;
    int sum = 0;
    int n =10;

    System.out.print(a+" "+b);
    for(int i=3;i<=n;i++)
    {
      sum = a + b;
      System.out.print(" "+sum);
      a = b;
      b = sum;
    }
  }
}
```

1.5 ARRAYS

We know that if we want to represent an integer variable, you will define it like this

int a1;

Similarly, if you want to represent a few more variables so it will be as below

int a1;

int a3 ;

int a4 ;

int a5 ;

int a6 ;

int a7 ;

int a8 ;

For the above variables, the memory will be allocated as below.

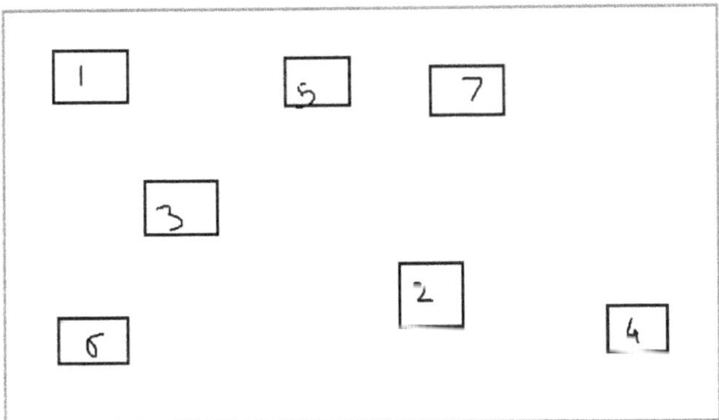

It will not be a continuous memory. Continuous memory is always better for retrieving the variable's values.

The Arrays in Java help us in that
now let's see what an array is

The array is a collection of similar types of elements located in continuous memory.

As shown in the diagram, a continuous memory is allocated to it when you create an Array. Array in java is defined as follows.

int[] a = new int[6];
The above array is of type integer, and its size is 6.

always remember that the indexing of the array starts from 0. (means numbering the location of elements)

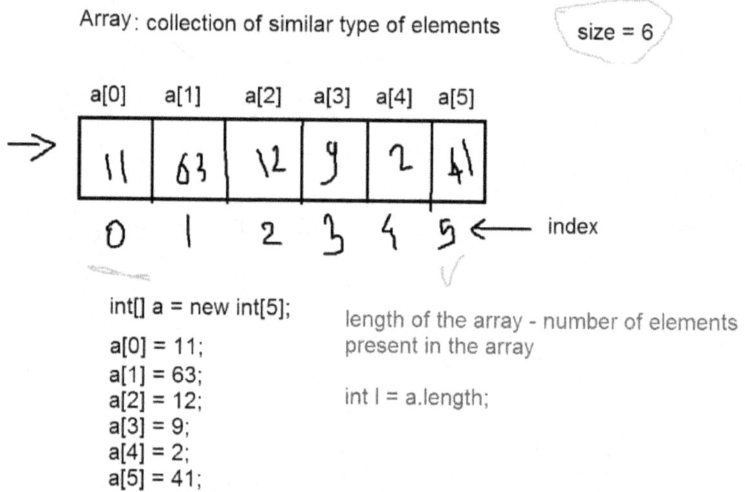

so if you want to store some elements in an array, you can store them as below

int[] a = new int[6]; (defining an array)

Storing values into an array

```
a[0] = 11;
a[1] = 63;
a[2] = 12;
a[3] = 9;
a[4] = 2;
a[5] = 41;
```

Now, if you want to print the value of the array at a particular index, you can print it as follows.

System.out.println(a[1]); this will print the value of an array at index 1;

If you want to print all the values of an array, you can print it using for loop as below.

Note: The length of an array means we can retrieve a total number of elements in an array with 'a.length.' where a is the name of an array.

```
for(int i=0;i<a.length ;i++)
    System.out.println(a[i]);
```

so the whole program of creating an array assigning values to it, and printing the array is as follows

```
public class ArrayDemo {
    public static void main(String[] args) {

        int[]  a = new int[6];

        a[0] = 11;
        a[1] = 63;
        a[2] = 12;
        a[3] = 9;
        a[4] = 2;
        a[5] = 41;
```

```
      for(int i=0;i<a.length ;i++)
         System.out.println(a[i]);
   }
}
```

There is one more way to assign a value to the array as follows.

```
int[] a = {3,4,12,21,43,12,34,65,423,1};
```

the complete program below

```
public class ArrayDemo2 {
   public static void main(String[] args) {

      int[] a = {3,4,12,21,43,12,34,65,423,1};

      for(int i=0;i<a.length;i++)
         System.out.println(a[i]);
   }
}
```

I have shown you an array of type int; you can also have the array of any other type.

like float, double, char, String

one example of an array of a character as below

```
public class ArrayCharacter {

   public static void main(String[] args) {

      char[] chAr = new char[5];

      chAr[0] ='s';
      chAr[1] ='d';
      chAr[2] ='f';
      chAr[3] ='#';
      chAr[4] ='!';
```

```java
        for(int i=0;i<chAr.length;i++)
            System.out.println(chAr[i]);



    }
}
```

Another example

```java
public class ArrayAnotherWay2 {

    public static void main(String[] args) {

        char[] a = {'v','f','o','#'};

        for(int i=0; i<a.length ; i++)
            System.out.print(a[i]+" ");

        System.out.println("\ndecmial values array");

        float f = 1.4f;
        double d = 1.4; // it has double the range of the float

        double[] dArray = {12.3,13.2,24.3,35.2,11.6,22.6};
        for (int i=0;i<dArray.length;i++)
            System.out.print(dArray[i]+" ");



    }
}
```

Two dimensional arrays

int[] a = new int[5]

	0	1	2	3	4
0	11	63	22	21	18

Single dimentional array is a single row array

two dimentional array is multi row array

int[][] a = new int[row][col];

row x col	0	1	2
0	0,0	0,1	0,2
1	1,0	1,1	1,2
2	2,0	2,1	2,2
3	3,0	3,1	3,2
4	4,0	4,1	4,2

it has rows and columns (in the array, mention row first, then column)

consider below example

int[][] a = new int[4][3];

here an array of size rows 4 and column 3 is defined & if you want to set some values into it, you can set it as follows

a[0][0] = 34;
a[0][1] = 36;
a[0][2] = 26;

a[1][0] = 14;
a[1][1] = 16;
a[1][2] = 56;

a[2][0] = 31;
a[2][1] = 32;
a[2][2] = 21;

a[3][0] = 36;
a[3][1] = 31;
a[3][2] = 76;

We know that we can get the length of the single-dimensional array with 'a.length.' Here, for 2-dimensional arrays, we have rows and columns & we can get the values of rows and columns as follows.

int row = a.length;
int col = a[0].length;

to print the array, we will need 2 for loops as below

```
for(int i=0;i<a.length;i++) {

  for (int j=0;j<a[0].length;j++)  {
      System.out.print(a[i][j]+" ");
  }
  System.out.println();
}
```

1. The outer for loop traverse for the rows
2. inner for loop traverse for the column
3. say the outer for loop is at index 0, then the inner for loop will traverse all the column-like
   0,0 ; 0,1 ; 0,2; ...... etc
   - here we should consider 3 points
   - While printing in an inner for loop, the println method is written just as print; it avoids new lines. We want all the same column numbers to be printed on the same line.
   - Then we have kept or attached space with each number so that the following number should not stick to the previous number.
   - outside the inner for loop there is **System.*out*.println();**

This is for printing a new line after printing all column values in a row.

so below is the complete program

```java
public class TwoDimentionalArray {
  public static void main(String[] args) {

    int[][] a = new int[4][3];

    a[0][0] = 34;
    a[0][1] = 36;
    a[0][2] = 26;

    a[1][0] = 14;
    a[1][1] = 16;
    a[1][2] = 56;

    a[2][0] = 31;
    a[2][1] = 32;
    a[2][2] = 21;

    a[3][0] = 36;
    a[3][1] = 31;
    a[3][2] = 76;

    int row  = a.length;
    int col = a[0].length;

    System.out.println("row="+row);
    System.out.println("col="+col);

    for(int i=0;i<a.length;i++)
    {
       for (int j=0;j<a[0].length;j++)
       {
          System.out.print(a[i][j]+" ");
       }
       System.out.println();
    }
```

```
    }
}
```

There is one more way to set values to the two-dimensional array. Let's understand this with the help of the below example..

```
int[][] a = {
      {1,1,1},
      {2,2,2},
      {3,3,3},
      {4,4,4},
      {5,5,5}
};
```

As we have already mentioned, the 2-dimensional array is the array of multiple single-dimensional arrays, so the above is one more method to set the values to the array.

Again remember that we have seen above 2 examples of 2-dimensional arrays of 'int' datatype.

You can have the 2-Dimensional arrays of other types, like float, double, char, String, etc.

1.6 STRINGS

The String is generally a character sequence; in java, it is a class. The String is defined like,

String str = "myString";

To find the length of a string, use the length() function.

So **str.length()** will give me 8 as a string length.

Like array string also has an index which starts with 0,

to find characters at a specific index use **charAt(i)** function where i is the index of the character.

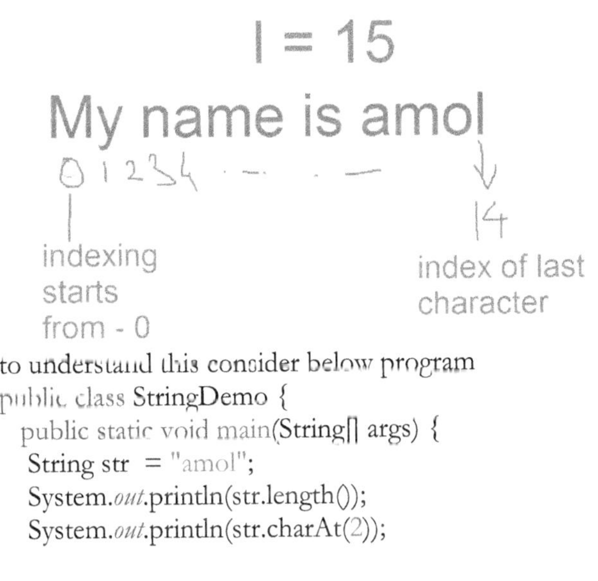

to understand this consider below program

```java
public class StringDemo {
   public static void main(String[] args) {
     String str  = "amol";
     System.out.println(str.length());
     System.out.println(str.charAt(2));
```

```
    String str1="this is a java";
    // find character at 3 & length
    System.out.println("str1 length="+str1.length());
System.out.println("char at index 3="+str1.charAt(3));
 }
}
```

So for you below is one exercise do it for practice

```
String str2="hi i am here";
// find character at index 2  & length
String str3="where are you";
// find character at index 0 &  length
String str4="this is a demo";
// find character at index 5 & length
String str5="core java";
// find character at index 6 & length
```

Now lets see some more methods in string.

1. toUpperCase() : - it converts the given string into uppercase
2. toLowerCase() : - it converts the given string into lower case

Below is an example of a program

```
public class JavaPrograms {
public static void main(String[] args)
{
 String str1="this is a java";
 String str2="HI I AM VIPUL";
 System.out.println("Str1 is:'"+str1+"'");
 System.out.println("Str1                              in
lower          case:'"+str1.toUpperCase()+"'");
 System.out.println("Str2 is:'"+str2+"'");
 System.out.println("Str2 in lower case:'"+str2.toLowerCase()+"'");
}
}
```

output :
Str1 is:'this is a java'
Str1 in lower case:'THIS IS A JAVA'
Str2 is:'HI I AM VIPUL'
Str2 in lower case:'hi i am vipul'

Substring - substring is a part of a string. For example, consider the below String.

String str = "this is a java class";
The examples of a substring of this String would be
'this' , 'is' , 'java' , 'is a java' , 'ava cla'
there are 2 ways to get the substring

1. str.substring(i) - i is the index
staring from ith index character till the end of the String
(ith index character is inclusive)

2. str.substring(beginIndex,endIndex) - starting with beginIndex
(beginIndex is inclusive) till the endIndex(endIndex is not inclusive)
Consider the below program. For example

```java
public class mySubString {
public static void main(String[] args)
{
        String str="this is ajava";
        System.out.println(str.substring(3));
        System.out.println(str.substring(3,9));
}
}
```

output :
s is ajava
s is a

Another essential function of String is 'split.' its syntax is str.split("ch
"). it will return an array of a string split by the character you specify
inside the split. Let's understand this with the help of an example.

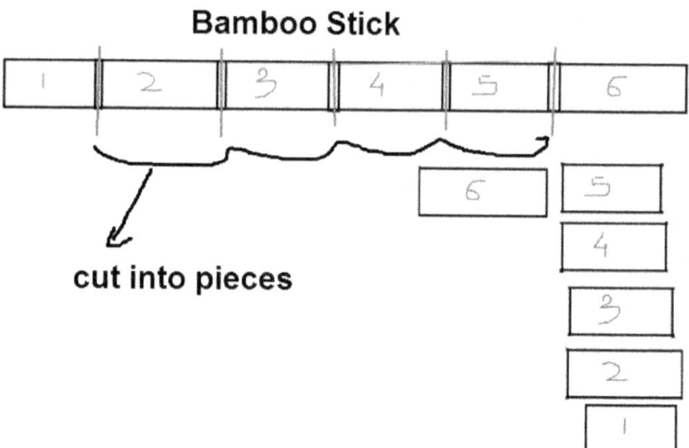

Consider a bamboo stick. We know that every bamboo stick has some markings, as shown. Let's assume that you have been told to cut that bamboo stick from its marking. so, after the cut, we can observe below two things

1.   we got a set of multiple small sticks
2.   the marking has vanished

Now consider another example
String str = "we are in a java class"

We have a method that can split this String. It is
split("character sequence"): the character sequence can be a single character or multiple continuous characters.

for example, space
str.split(" "); → this will split the String with space, and again you can see below two observations

1.   we got a set of multiple strings
2.   the space has vanished

the split method returns an array of a string, so let's store this into an array, like below

String[] stArr = str.split(" ");

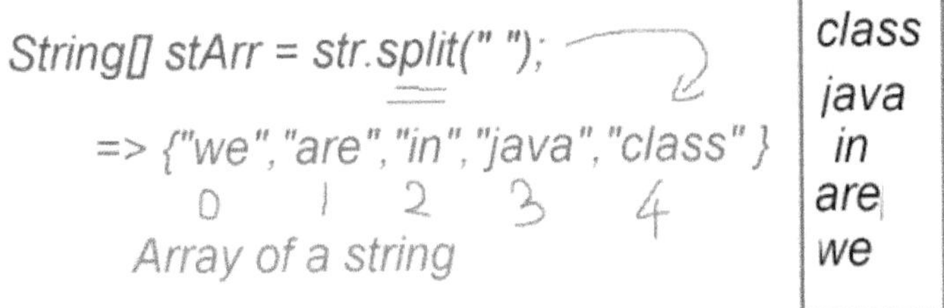

now if you want to print this array, we can do it using for loop

```
for(int i =0; i< stArr.length;i++)
        System.out.println(stArr[i]);
```

output:

we

are

in

java

class

String Comparison

generally, while comparing 2 data types, we use == symbol, for example, a == b. It returns a true or false value.

Since String is a class and a string variable is a class object, we can't compare it with == symbol. Below is the way to compare the two Strings.

String str1 = "Amol"

String str2 = "Amol"

str1.equals(str2); → this returns true or false value, here it is true

now consider the below example

String str1 = "amol",

String str2 = "amol";

String str3 = "Amol";

String str4 = "xyz";

String str5 = "PQR";

String str6 = new String("amol");

here we have,
str1.equals(str2); → true (Strings are equal)
str1.equals(str3); → false (A is capital)
str1.equals(str4); → false(complete different strings)
str1.equals(str6); → true (Strings are equal)

If all the characters in the strings are the same, some character cases are different. If you want to compare them by ignoring the case, below is the method.

str1.equalsIgnoreCase(str3); → now this will be true

Fine, now the question arises if I compare strings with == symbol then what will happen, the answer is, it will compare two strings address so

str1 == str2 will compare the address of 2 string , now we know
String str1 = "Amol"
String str2 = "Amol"

So str1 == str2 because it is comparing the two addresses, the result of comparison should be false, so ideally, it should give me false as a result upon printing.

but if you run this
System.*out*.println(str1==str2);

you will see it is printing true. why ?

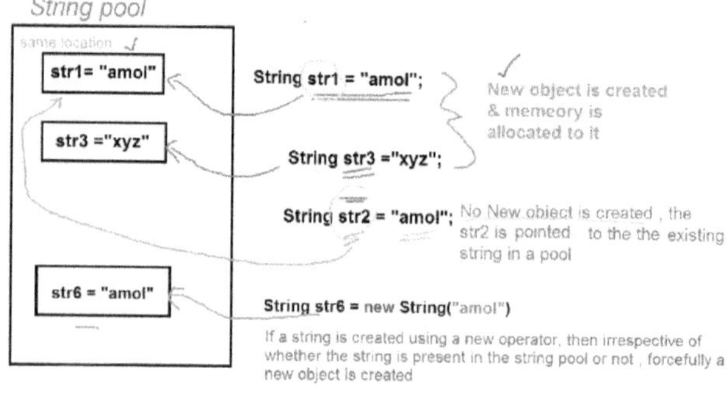

See the above diagram. In this, a string pool or a memory is shown. When a variable is created, memory is allocated to it. So when the str1 variable is created, a memory gets allocated to it. We assign a value as "amol" to it. Still, when another variable is created, we give again "amol" to it a new memory is not created. The variable is pointed to the old location where the string "amol" is in the string pool.

now when you create a string variable (object) using a new operator, forcefully, a new object is created, and a separate memory is allocated to it, irrespective of whether it has the same String or not

```
String str6 = new String("amol");
→ new object / memory is created here
public class StringComparison {
    public static void main(String[] args) {
        String str1 = "amol";
        String str2 = "amol";
        String str3 = "Amol";
        String str4 = "xyz";
        String str5 = "PQR";
        String str6 = new String("amol");

        int a =10 ;
        int b =20;
        System.out.println(a==b);

        System.out.println(str1.equals(str2));
        // true

        System.out.println(str1.equals(str3));
        // false

        System.out.println(str1.equalsIgnoreCase(str3));
        // true

        System.out.println(str1.equals(str4));
        // false

        System.out.println(str1.equals(str6));
        // false
```

```java
System.out.println(str1==str2); // true
System.out.println(str1==str6); // false

    }
}
```

1.7 DATE

As a string, Date is also a class & the date variable is defined below.

Date date = new Date();

now, if you print the 'date' variable, you will get the current system date printed as below

> Date date = new Date();
> System.*out*.println(date);
>
> output :
> Tue Apr 13 07:49:13 IST 2021

Above is the current system date. We don't have a habit of seeing the date in this format. We generally know the date as like, 13/04/2021 or 12-02-2019 like this.

Now can we convert the above date into this format? Yes, we can. The above form ('Tue Apr 13 07:49:13 IST 2021) is the date object format or a system formatted date, and we can convert it into a string using a class simple date format. We have to provide the pattern you want this date to be converted into a String. as below.

```
SimpleDateFormat sd = new
SimpleDateFormat("dd/MM/yyyy");
```

SimpleDateFormat is a class, and "dd/MM/yyyy" is the pattern with which we are supposed to get the String, so after this, you have to write.

```
sd.format(Date);
```

now either assign this to a string variable or print/use it directly. The same is done in the program below.

```java
import java.text.SimpleDateFormat;
import java.util.Date;
public class DateDemo {
    public static void main(String[] args) {

        Date date = new Date();
        System.out.println(date);

        SimpleDateFormat sd = new
SimpleDateFormat("dd/MM/yyyy");

        String dateStr = sd.format(date);

        // converted Date into String
        System.out.println(sd.format(date)); // or
        System.out.println(dateStr);
    }
}
```

Below is the table where different notations & their meaning is given to be used for creating patterns

Notation	Description	Example
dd	day in digit	02
E /EE / EEE	day in words (partial)	Mon
EEEE	day in words (Full)	Monday
MM (m capital)	Month in digit	03
MMM	Month in words (partial)	Mar
MMMM	Month in words (Full)	March
M	Month in a single digit when month is single digit. (if we use MM then it gives 02 otherwise 2)	2
yy	year in 2 digit	16
yyyy	year in 4 digit	2016
hh	hours (24 hour clock)	11
mm	minutes	23
ss	Seconds	11

Now consider below string patterns

1. String dateStr1= "23 | June 16 8:34"
2. String dateStr2= "2016 - 06 - 23 | 8:34:23"
3. String dateStr3= "Thursday 2016/06/23"
4. String dateStr4= "23-06-2016 | thu | 8:34"
5. String dateStr5= "8:34:22"

let's convert the current date in these patterns; below is the complete program (while identifying the pattern, the above table is taken into consideration)

```java
import java.text.SimpleDateFormat;
import java.util.Date;

public class DateDemo1 {
  public static void main(String[] args) {
      Date date = new Date();
      System.out.println(date);

      SimpleDateFormat sd1
      = new SimpleDateFormat("dd | MMMM yy h:mm");

      String dateStr1 = sd1.format(date);
      System.out.println(dateStr1);

      SimpleDateFormat sd2
      = new SimpleDateFormat("yyyy - MM - dd | h:mm:ss");

      String dateStr2 = sd2.format(date);
      System.out.println(dateStr2);


      SimpleDateFormat sd3
      = new SimpleDateFormat("EEEE yyyy/MM/dd");
      String dateStr3 = sd3.format(date);

      System.out.println(dateStr3);

      SimpleDateFormat sd4
         = new SimpleDateFormat("dd-MM-yyyy | E | h:mm");

      String dateStr4 = sd4.format(date);
      System.out.println(dateStr4);

      SimpleDateFormat sd5
         = new SimpleDateFormat("h:mm:ss");
```

```java
        String dateStr5 = sd5.format(date);
        System.out.println(dateStr5);
    }
}
```

output :
```
Thu Apr 15 07:24:44 IST 2021
15 | April 21 7:24
2021 - 04 - 15 | 7:24:44
Thursday 2021/04/15
15-04-2021 | Thu | 7:24
7:24:44
```

Now, suppose you have a string that represents a date,
String dateStr = "10/04/2019";
If you want to convert this into a date, then below are the steps

1. identified the pattern of the date in a string (here it is dd/MM/yyyy)
2. create a SimpleDateFormat object with this patten
3. use the method parse with the object to convert this String.

see the below program to understand this

```java
import java.text.SimpleDateFormat;
import java.util.Date;

public class StringToDate {

    public static void main(String[] args) throws ParseException {

        String dateStr = "10/27/2021"; // MM/dd/yyyy
        System.out.println(dateStr);

        SimpleDateFormat sd = new SimpleDateFormat("MM/dd/yyyy");

        Date date = sd.parse(dateStr);
```

```
        System.out.println(date);
        System.out.println(sd.parse(dateStr));
    }
}
```

output :
10/27/2021
Wed Oct 27 00:00:00 IST 2021

Now consider below strings
  1. String dateStr1= "23 | June 16 8:34"
  2. String dateStr2= "2016 - 06 - 23 | 8:34:23"
  3. String dateStr3= "Thursday 2016/06/23"
  4. String dateStr4= "23-06-2016 | thu | 8:34"
  5. String dateStr5= "8:34:22"

convert these strings into date
Below is the program


```java
import java.text.ParseException;
import java.text.SimpleDateFormat;

public class StringToDate1 {
  public static void main(String[] args) throws ParseException {

    String dateStr1= "23 | June 16  8:34";
    // => dd | MMMM yy hh:mm
    SimpleDateFormat sd1
        = new SimpleDateFormat("dd | MMMM yy hh:mm");
    System.out.println(sd1.parse(dateStr1));

    String dateStr2= "2016 - 06 - 23 | 8:34:23";
    // yyyy - MM - dd | h:mm:ss
    SimpleDateFormat sd2
        = new SimpleDateFormat("yyyy - MM - dd | h:mm:ss");
    System.out.println(sd2.parse(dateStr2));
```

```java
String dateStr3= "Thursday 2016/06/23";
//EEEE yyyy/MM/dd
SimpleDateFormat sd3
  = new SimpleDateFormat("EEEE yyyy/MM/dd");
System.out.println(sd3.parse(dateStr3));

String dateStr4= "23-06-2016 | thu | 8:34";
// dd-MM-yyyy | E | h:mm
SimpleDateFormat sd4
    = new SimpleDateFormat("dd-MM-yyyy | E | h:mm");
System.out.println(sd4.parse(dateStr4));

String dateStr5= "8:34:22";
// h:mm:ss
SimpleDateFormat sd5 = new SimpleDateFormat("h:mm:ss");
System.out.println(sd5.parse(dateStr5));
  }
}
```

So key takeaways are,
1. to convert Date into String, use format method (Remember this word FDS - abbreviated as use format → date to String)
2. to convert String into a date, use the parse method (Remember this word PSD - abbreviated as use Parse → String to Date)

1.8 CLASSES AND CONSTRUCTORS

Since we have started learning java, every program we are creating into a class. So what is this class?

A class contains data members and member functions.

Data members can be any data type, string, or date object.

for example
int a;
double d;
char c;
String str

Member functions which are also known as methods
it can be as below

void display()
{
  some body.
}

now consider the below points
1. we can not access data members or member functions directly in the main function
2. to access them, we need to create an object of the class (object is also known as an instance of a class)
3. Objection creation is shown below

ClassName objectName = new ClassName();

objectName.a = 10; (int this way we can access the data members)

let us see one program to understand this

```java
public class MyClass {
    int a;
    float f;
    char c;
    String str; // data members

    void display() // member function
    {
        System.out.println("a="+a);
        System.out.println("f="+f);
        System.out.println("c="+c);
        System.out.println("str="+str);
    }

    public static void main(String[] args) {
        MyClass ob = new MyClass();
        ob.a = 10 ;
        ob.f = 6.4f;
        ob.c = 'n';
        ob.str = "amol";
            ob.display();
    }
}
```

Output :
a=10
f=6.4
c=n
str=amol

Now we have recently said that an object is also known as an instance of a class, which means that whenever we create an object, it will have a separate memory block for it, that that memory block will be the instance of the class

ob1 →

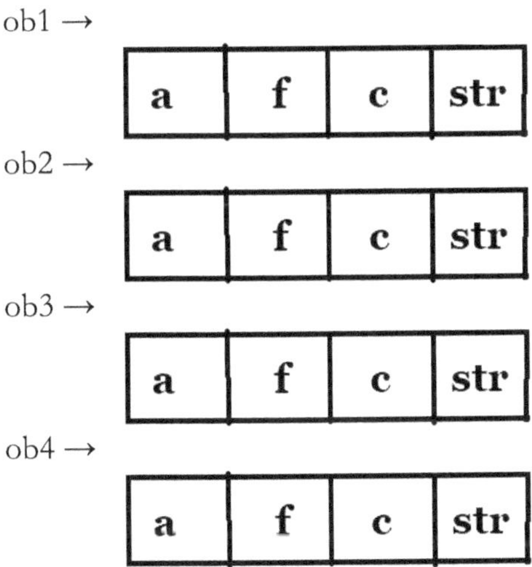

ob2 →

ob3 →

ob4 →

Below is an example of how we can create different objects

```
MyClass ob1 = new MyClass();
ob1.a = 11 ;
ob1.f = 7.4f;
ob1.c = '7';
ob1.str = "sonali";
ob1.display();

MyClass ob2 = new MyClass();
ob2.a = 21 ;
ob2.f = 70.4f;
ob2.c = 'k';
ob2.str = "sunny";
ob2.display();
```

So the thing to be understood is that ob1.a is different, and ob2.a is different.

Constructors :

1. constructors are used to initializing the objects
2. it has the same name as that of a class name
3. it is a method with no return type
4. for example, if below is the class

class MyClass
{
}

Then Constructor for it would be

```
MyClass()
{
  // body of a constructor.
}
```

1. **Default constructor:** when no constructor is defined inside a class, a default constructor is invoked and initializes the object.

example below :

```
public class MyClassDemo2 {
  int a;
  float f;
  char c;
  String str; // data members

  void display() // member function
  {
    System.out.println("a="+a);
    System.out.println("f="+f);
    System.out.println("c="+c);
    System.out.println("str="+str);
  }
  public static void main(String[] args) {
    MyClassDemo2 ob  =new MyClassDemo2();
    ob.display();
  }
}
```
output :
a=0

f=0.0
c=
str=null
(the initialization of the members to, 0,0.0, blank & null; is done by a default constructor)

2. Empty Constructor: when a constructor is defined with no body, it is known as an empty Constructor. It does the same effect as that of the default constructor.

example below :

```java
public class MyClassDemo2 {
   int a;
   float f;
   char c;
   String str; // data members

       MyClassDemo2()
          {
            // no body - empty constructor

          }

   void display() // member function
     {
       System.out.println("a="+a);
       System.out.println("f="+f);
       System.out.println("c="+c);
       System.out.println("str="+str);
     }
   public static void main(String[] args) {
      MyClassDemo2 ob  =new MyClassDemo2();
      ob.display();
    }
}
```
output :
a—0
f=0.0
c=
str=null

(the initialization of the members to, 0,0.0, blank & null; is done by an empty constructor)

3. Constructor: when a constructor is defined but with body and data members being initialized inside it, it is known as a Constructor.

example below :

```java
public class MyClassWithConst {
    int a;
    float f;
    char c;
    String str; // data members

    MyClassWithConst()
    {
        a =10 ;
        f = 3.4f;
        c ='g';
        str="amol";
    }

    void display() // member function
    {
        System.out.println("a="+a);
        System.out.println("f="+f);
        System.out.println("c="+c);
        System.out.println("str="+str);
    }

    public static void main(String[] args) {

        MyClassWithConst ob  =new MyClassWithConst();
        ob.display();
    }
}
```
output :
a=10
f=3.4
c=g

str=amol

(the initialization of the members to, 10,3.4, g & amol; is done by Constructor)

4. Parameterized Constructor: Here, the data members' values are set through the parameters passed to the Constructor.

example below :

```java
public class MyClassParmConst {
   int a;
   float f;
   char c;
   String str; // data members

   MyClassParmConst(int x,float ff,char ch,String s)
   {
      a = x ;
      f = ff;
      c = ch;
      str = s;
   }

   void display() // member function
   {

      System.out.println("a="+a);
      System.out.println("f="+f);
      System.out.println("c="+c);
      System.out.println("str="+str);
   }

   public static void main(String[] args) {

   MyClassParmConst ob
         =new MyClassParmConst(23,4.5f,'d',"abcd");
      ob.display();
   }
}
```

output :

a=23
f=4.5
c=d
str=abcd
(the initialization of the members to, 23,4.5, d & abcd; is done by parameterized Constructor)

5. Parameterized Constructor with 'this' operator: to bring ease into coding, in Constructor, the parameter is given the same name as data members. We know that parameter variables are always local variables now. To identify the current object data members, we use this operator with a dot along with a data member name (inside the Constructor)

example below :

```java
public class MyClassParmConstThis {
   int a;
   float f;
   char c;
   String str; // data members

   MyClassParmConstThis(int a, float f , char c , String str)
   {
      this.a =  a;
      this.f = f;
      this.c = c;
      this.str = str;
   }


   void display() // member function
   {
      System.out.println("a="+a);
      System.out.println("f="+f);
      System.out.println("c="+c);
      System.out.println("str="+str);
   }

   public static void main(String[] args) {
```

```
MyClassParmConstThis ob
    =new MyClassParmConstThis(23,4.5f,'d',"abcd");

ob.display();


    }


    }
```

output :
a=23
f=4.5
c=d
str=abcd
(the initialization of the members to , 23,4.5, d & abcd ; is done by parameterized constructor with this operator)

Access Modifiers :

Access modifiers define the scope of your data member or member function. Scope means accessibility. Now to understand these, let's do one activity.

pack1 — Java1
pack1 — Java2
pack2 — Java3
pack2 — Java4

```
public class Java1 {
    int a1;
    float f1;
    char c1;
    String str1; // data members

    void display1() // member function
    {
        System.out.println("a="+a1);
        System.out.println("f="+f1);
        System.out.println("c="+c1);
        System.out.println("str="+str1);
    }

    public static void main(String[] args) {
    }

}
```

1. Create two packages (pack1 & pack2) - by the way, the package is nothing but just like a folder created in the src folder of your project.
2. In each package, create two java classes, name them Java1, Java2 (in pack1), and Java3, Java4 (in pack2).
3. create a java class with some data members and a member function in each class (as shown in the diagram)
4. Just do one thing if it is a Java1 (class) then keep postfix of data member / member function as 1, for e.g. a1,c1, display1(), if it is Java2 (class) then keep postfix of data member / member function as 2, for e.g. a2,c2, display2() & so on.

now we will perform a particular operation
- Remember when you don't provide/write any access
- modifier before the variable/method declaration. Its access modifier is 'default.'
- other than the default, there are access modifiers like public, private, protected

Case :1.1

-------------------- Pack1.Java1-------------
public static void main(String[] args) {

```
Java1 ob = new Java1();
ob.a1 = 10;
ob.f1 =4.5f;
ob.c1 = 'g';
ob.display1();
}
```

- The above main function is written in the class Java1, which is in pack1
- I have created an object of Java1 & using this object. I am trying to access the default members (no access modifier is written)
- I can comfortably access it.

- It means we can access default members **from the same class**.

Case :1.2

------------------- Pack1.Java2---------------

```
public static void main(String[] args) {

    Java1 ob = new Java1();
    ob.a1 = 10;
    ob.f1 =4.5f;
    ob.c1 = 'g';
    ob.display1();
}
```

- The above main function is written in the class Java2, which is in pack1
- I have created an object of Java1 & using this object. I am trying to access the default members (no access modifier is written)
- I can comfortably access it.
- We can access default members from **other classes in the same package**.

Case :1.3

------------------- Pack 2.Java 3--------------

```
public static void main(String[] args) {

    Java1 ob = new Java1();

    ob.a1 =78;
    ob.str1 = "str";
    ob.f1 =4.5f;
    ob.display1();
}
```

- The above main function is written in the class Java3, which is in pack2.
- I have created an object of Java1 & using this object. I am trying to access the default members (no access modifier is written)
- I can't access it
- We can not access default members **from other classes outside the package.**

Conclusion
we can access default members in
- Same class
- Another class in the same package
- Can not be accessed another class in another package

Now, if you make the members **public**, we can access them
- In same class
- Another class in the same package
- another class in another package
- you have to write the keyword public before it


```java
public class Java1 {

    public int a1;
    public  float f1;
    public  char c1;
    public String str1; // data members

    public  void display1() // member function
    {
        System.out.println("a="+a1);
        System.out.println("f="+f1);
        System.out.println("c="+c1);
        System.out.println("str="+str1);
    }
}
```


If a member is private then understand **we can access private members-only** within the same class.

Case 1 : (same class - accessible)

```java
public class Java1 {

  public int a1;
  public  float f1;
  private char c1;
  public String str1;  // data members

  public  void display1()  // member function
  {
     System.out.println("a="+a1);
     System.out.println("f="+f1);
     System.out.println("c="+c1);
     System.out.println("str="+str1);
  }

  public static void main(String[] args) {

     Java1 ob = new Java1();
     ob.a1 = 10;
     ob.f1 =4.5f;
     ob.c1 = 'g';// Accessible
     ob.display1();
  }

}
```

Case 2 : (Another class same package - Not accessible)
---------------- pack1.Java2 ----------------------

```java
public class Java2{

  public static void main(String[] args) {

     Java1 ob = new Java1();
     ob.a1 =10;
     ob.f1 =4.5f;
     ob.c1 ='c'; // not accessible
     ob.display1();
```

```
    }

}
```

Case 3 : (Another class another package - Not accessible)

```
----------------- pack2.Java3 ----------------------
public class Java3{

    public static void main(String[] args) {

        Java1 ob = new Java1();
        ob.a1 =10;
        ob.f1 =4.5f;
        ob.c1 ='c'; // not accessible
        ob.display1();

    }

}
```

There is one more access modifier protected, but to understand that, we need to learn the inheritance first, so let's know about inheritance in the next chapter.

1.9 INHERITANCE

In the last chapter, you might have observed that we can create an object of one class into another, but I can access only the same class members using this object.

Now I am going to introduce a concept with which we will create objects of one class & will access the members of some other class with the help of Inheritance.

for that, you will have to create
1. one class with some members, let this class be a parent class (also known as a super class or base class)
2. and we will create another class, let that class be the child class (also known as a subclass or derived class)

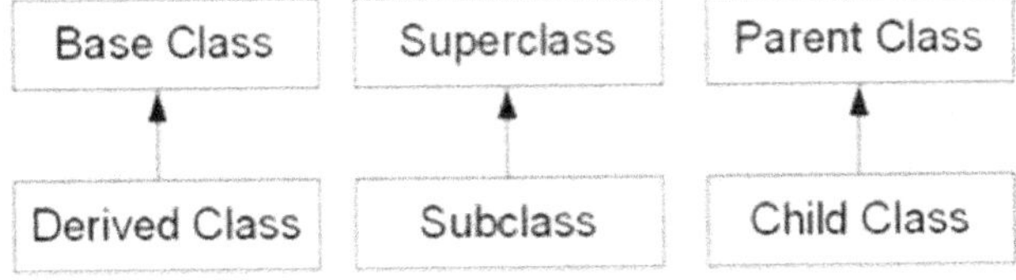

* **Inheritance:** Inheritance can be defined as a process in which one class (child class) can acquire properties (fields and methods) of another class (parent class).

- **Parent Class:** The class whose properties are inherited is called parent class or base class or superclass.
- **Child Class:** The class which inherits the properties of others is called child class or derived class, or subclass.

let's see one example below

```java
public class BaseClass {

   int a;

   double d;

   void method1()

   {

      System.out.println("this is method 1");

   }

}


class DerivedClass extends BaseClass

{

   char c;

   String str;

   void method2()

   {

      System.out.println("this is method 2");

   }


   public static void main(String[] args) {

      DerivedClass ob = new DerivedClass();

      ob.c = 'g';

      ob.str ="amol";

      ob.method2();
```

```
    ob.a = 10;

    ob.d = 2.3;

    ob.method1();

  }

}
```

In the above example, we can see using the child class object. We can access not only its members but also the parent class members.

there is one base class & one derived class, so this is known as Single Inheritance

There are different types of inheritances.

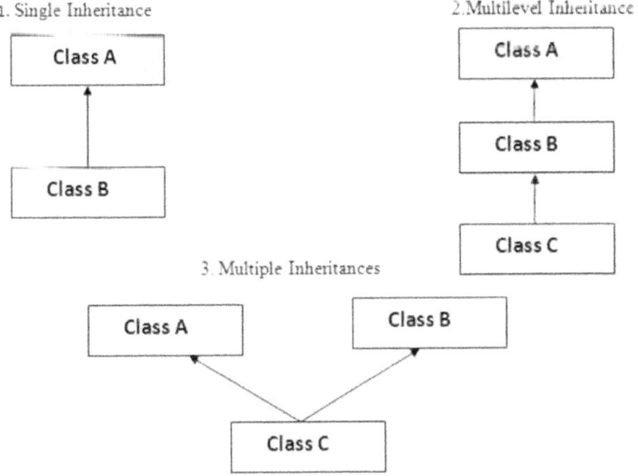

4. Hierarchical Inheritances

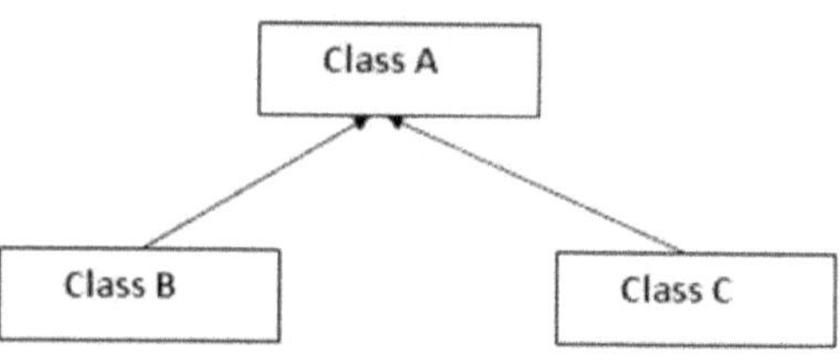

5. Hybrid inheritance:

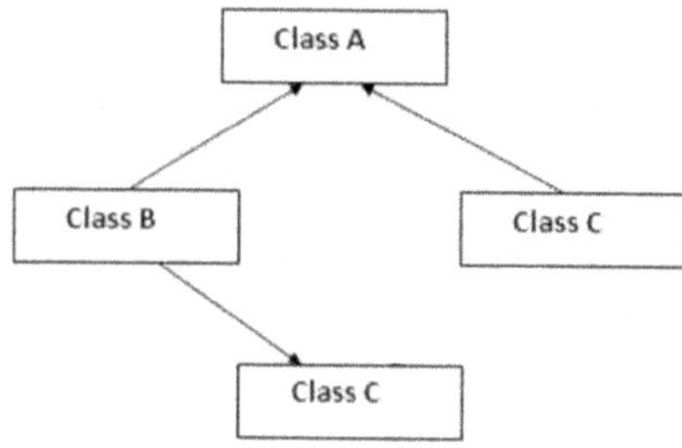

Multilevel Inheritance

In this case, there is one base class with a derived class. And again, there is one more derived class which is the child of the second class & so on. this kind of Inheritance is known as multilevel Inheritance.

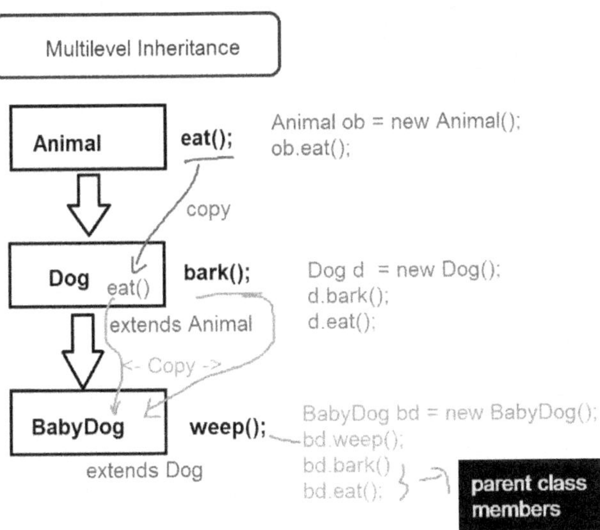

Consider the above example here, an Animal. A base class is a base class, who has a child class as Dog & again Dog has child class Babydog

1. The Animal class has one method, eat(), so its child class object Dog can access it using its object. The reason is that one copy of eat() goes into the class Dog.
2. So the class Dog has a method bark(), and its child class object BabyDog can access it.
3. BabyDog's object can also access the method eat(), which belongs to the class Animal because, for the same reason, a copy of eat() is there in the class dog. So in the class 'Babydog', a copy of eat() & bark() is there.

```java
public class Animal {

    void eat()
    {
        System.out.println("eat()");
    }

}
```

```java
class Dog extends Animal
{
  void barks()
  {
    System.out.println("Barks()");
  }
}

class  BabyDog extends  Dog
{
  void weeps()
  {
    System.out.println("weeps()");
  }
}

class TestInheritance
{
  public static void main(String[] args) {

    Animal animal = new Animal();
    animal.eat();

    Dog dog = new Dog();
    dog.barks();
    dog.eat();

    BabyDog babyDog = new BabyDog();
    babyDog.weeps();
    babyDog.barks();
    babyDog.eat();

  }
}
```

Output:
eat()
Barks()
eat()
weeps()

Barks()
eat()

3. Multiple inheritance :

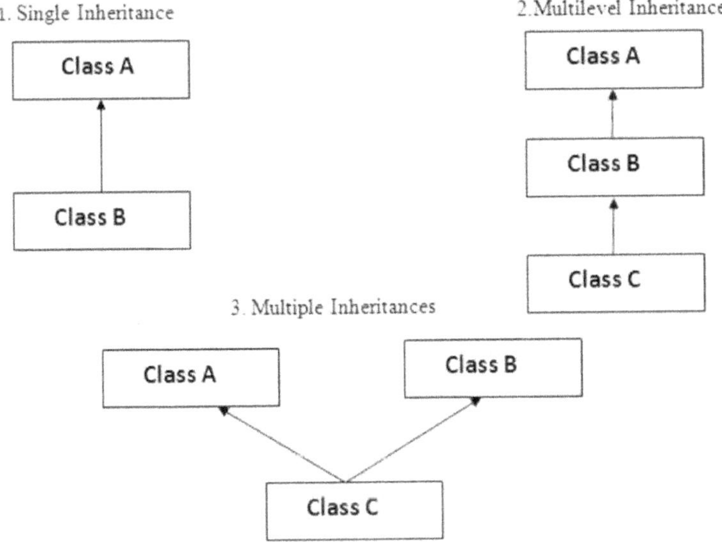

Above hierarchy is said to be a multiple inheritances where we have two or more base classes and only one derived class. This case is **not possible** in Java. The reason is as below

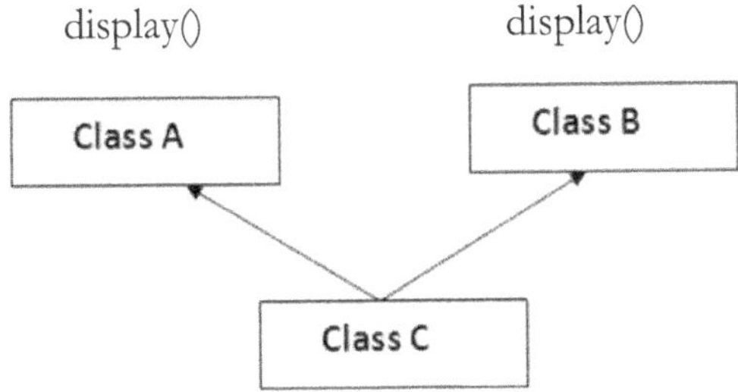

Suppose both the classes class A and class B have a method display();

Now, if I create the object of class C, then as per the definition of Inheritance, I can access the parent class members

so when I do this way

C ob = new C();

ob.display();

Now, this kind of ambiguity is created, and that is whose display method is to be called. So multiple Inheritance is not possible in Java.

4. Hierarchical Inheritance :

This type of Inheritance is known as Hierarchical Inheritance.

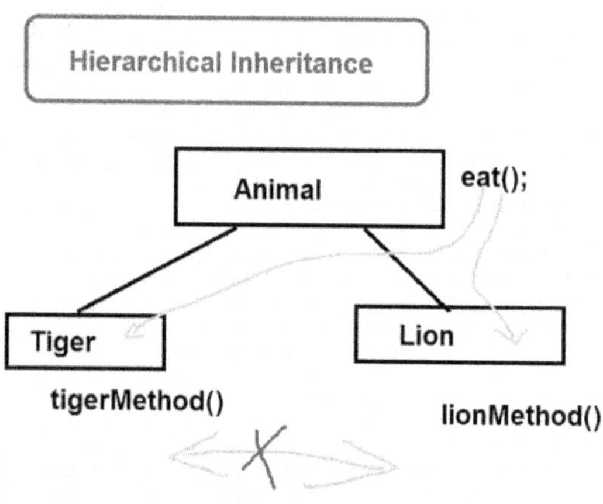

- In this example, Animal is the base class & it has two child classes: one is Tiger, and the other is Lion.
- Tiger has one method tigerMethod(), Lion has one method lionMethod().
- using the object of the Tiger, we can access its method that is the tigerMethod() and the eat() method, which belongs to its parent class
- Using another child that is the Lion using its object, we can access its method, the lineMethod(), and the method from its parent, that is, the eat() method.

Consider below example

public class Animal1 {

  void eat()

  {

```java
        System.out.println("eat");
  }

}

class Tiger extends Animal1
{
  void methodTiger()
  {
     System.out.println("Tiger Method");
  }
}

class Lion extends Animal1
{
  void methodLion()
  {
     System.out.println("Lion Method");
  }
}

class TestInheritance1
{
  public static void main(String[] args) {

     Animal1 ob = new Animal1();
     ob.eat();

     Tiger tiger = new Tiger();
```

```
        tiger.eat();
        tiger.methodTiger();

        Lion lion = new Lion();
        lion.eat();
        lion.methodLion();

    }
}
```

Output:

eat

eat

Tiger Method

eat

Lion Method

5. Hybrid Inheritance

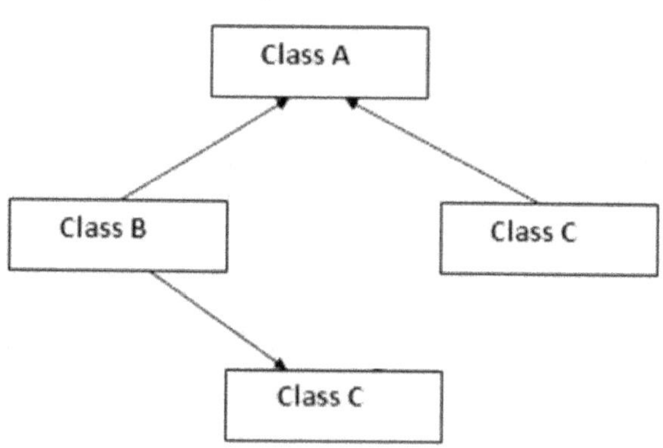

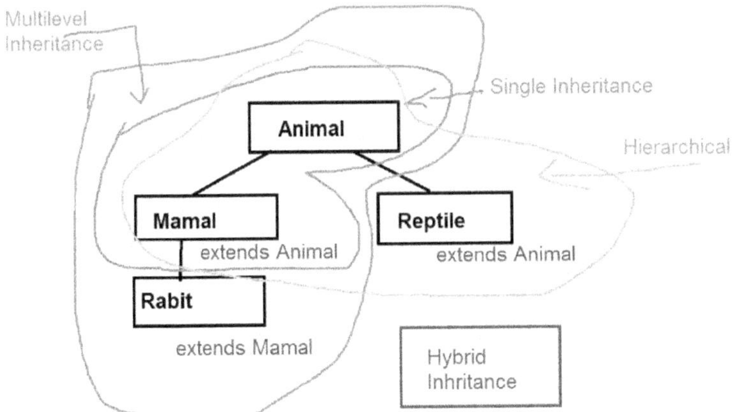

Consider the above example. In this example, we can observe different types of inheritances are implemented like single, multilevel, and hierarchical.

This kind of Inheritance is known as hybrid Inheritance.

Below is the program example

```java
public class Animal2 {
  void eat()
  {
    System.out.println("eat");
  }
}
class Mamal extends Animal
{
  void methodMamal()
  {
    System.out.println("methodMamal");
  }
```

```java
}

class Reptile extends Animal
{
  void methodReptile()
  {
    System.out.println("methodReptile");
  }
}

class Rabit extends Mamal
{
  void methodRabit()
  {
    System.out.println("methodRabit");
  }
}

class Testinheritance3
{
  public static void main(String[] args) {
    Animal2 ob = new Animal2();
    ob.eat();
    Mamal mamal = new Mamal();
    mamal.eat();
    mamal.methodMamal();
    Reptile reptile = new Reptile();
    reptile.eat();
```

```
        reptile.methodReptile();

        Rabit rabit = new Rabit();

        rabit.eat();

        rabit.methodRabit();

        rabit.methodMamal();

    }

}
```

Output :

eat

eat()

methodMamal

eat()

methodReptile

eat()

methodRabit

methodMamal

Super Keyword
We can use the super keyword with
    1.   data member
    2.   member function
    3.   constructor

Super with data member
consider below example :

consider below example :

```
public class Automation {

    int testcaseId =101;

}
```

```java
class Selenium extends Automation
{
  int testcaseId = 202;
  void printTestCaseId()
  {
    System.out.println(testcaseId); // 202
    System.out.println(super.testcaseId); // 101
  }
  public static void main(String[] args) {
    Selenium ob = new Selenium();
    ob.printTestCaseId();
  }
}
```

In this example, we can see a data member testcaseID is present in both parent class as well as child class
if I try to access it inside the child class method, it will refer to the child class testcaseID only
if you want to refer to the testcaseID from the parent class, use the super keyword (We can use this way inside the member functions only)

Super with Member function
consider below example :

```java
public class Cucumber {

  int x =10;
  void execute()
  {
    System.out.println("Executing cucumber");
  }
```

```
}

class Framework extends Cucumber
{
  void execute()
  {
    System.out.println("Executing Framework");
  }

  void displayExecution()
  {
    execute();
    super.execute();
    System.out.println(super.x);
  }
  public static void main(String[] args) {
    Framework framework = new Framework(10);
    framework.displayExecution();
  }
}
```

In this example, we can see a member function execute() is present in both parent class as well as child class
if I try to access it inside the child class method, it will refer to the child class execute() method only
if you want to refer to the execute() method from the parent class, use the super keyword (We can use this way inside the member functions only)

Super with Constructor

In Inheritance, when you create an object of a child class, you need to give a call to the parent class constructor as. Well, consider the below example wherein it is given. Using the super keyword, we can give a call to the parent class constructor.

```java
public class Cucumber {
    Cucumber()
    {
        System.out.println("Cucumber constructor");
    }
}

class Framework extends Cucumber
{
    Framework()
    {
        super();
        // this will call super class constructor
        System.out.println("framework constructor");
    }

    public static void main(String[] args) {
        Framework framework = new Framework();
    }
}
```

Output :

Cucumber constructor

framework constructor

Now, even if you still don't call the constructor, it will be given a call. Refer below program

```java
public class Cucumber {

  Cucumber()
  {
    System.out.println("Cucumber constructor");
  }
}


class Framework extends Cucumber
{
  Framework()
  {
    System.out.println("framework constructor");
  }

  public static void main(String[] args) {
    Framework framework = new Framework();
  }
}
```

Output :

Cucumber constructor

framework constructor

Protected Keyword
We have seen different access modifiers earlier, like public-private and default.

- we have seen private members cant be accessed in the same class
- default members can't access members outside the package
- Public members can access the members from the same package and different packages.

Suppose you want the default members to be accessed outside the package. In that case, we can do that through Inheritance by making that member protected.

1.10 METHODS RETURNING VALUES AND METHODS TAKING ARGUMENTS

Till now, we have seen only one form of a method as below

```
void my method()
{
    //statements;
}
```

After the method name (here, it is a method), there is an empty parenthesis. It tells us that this method will execute the statements inside it when called.

Now, this method is with empty parentheses, so it is called the method with no argument,

now just like this, we can have a method with the argument as well, and the argument can be

1. Single argument (int, float, char, double, string..)
2. multiple arguments

let's see some example

1. single argument method

```java
void printData(int x)
{
    System.out.println("x=" + x);
}
```

1. Multiple argument method

```java
void printAnotherData(int x, double d, String s) {
    System.out.println("x=" + x);
    System.out.println("d=" + d);
    System.out.println("s=" + s);
}
```

The argument can be an array As well
1. array as an argument (single-dimensional)

```java
void printArray(int[] a) {
    for (int i = 0; i < a.length; i++)
        System.out.println(a[i]);
}
```

2. array as an argument (Two dimensional)

```java
void printTwoDArray(String[][] stArr) {
    for (int i = 0; i < stArr.length; i++) {
        for (int j = 0; j < stArr[0].length; j++) {
            System.out.print(stArr[i][j] + " ");
        }
}
```

```
      System.out.println();
  }
}
```

Consider the below program to understand the working of these methods.

```
public class MethodsArguments {

   int a;
   double d;

   void getData() // no arguments
   {
      System.out.println("a=" + a);
      System.out.println("d=" + d);
   }

   void printData(int x)
   {
      System.out.println("x=" + x);
   }

   void printAnotherData(int x, double d, String s) {
      System.out.println("x=" + x);

      System.out.println("d=" + d);

      System.out.println("s=" + s);
   }
```

```java
void printArray(int[] a) {

    for (int i = 0; i < a.length; i++)

        System.out.println(a[i]);

}


void printTwoDArray(String[][] stArr) {

    for (int i = 0; i < stArr.length; i++) {

    for (int j = 0; j < stArr[0].length; j++)  {

        System.out.print(stArr[i][j] + " ");

        }

        System.out.println();

    }

}



public static void main(String[] args) {

    MethodsArguments ob = new MethodsArguments();

    ob.getData();

    ob.printData(10);

    ob.printAnotherData(12,3.4,"amol");


    int[] x = {2,4,12,543,67,89};

    ob.printArray(x);


        String[][] str = {
```

```
            {"abc1","pqr1","xyz1"},

            {"abc2","pqr2","xyz2"},

            {"abc3","pqr3","xyz3"},

            {"abc4","pqr4","xyz4"}

    };

    ob.printTwoDArray(str);

  }

}
```

consider below method

```
void display()
{


}
```

void is a return type of this method, actually
Void means nothing
It means the method returns nothing (does not return anything)

If the **return type** is other than void, it can be
1. **Primitive data type**: int, float, char, double, boolean
2. **Array** → Single dimensional / 2 dimensional
3. **Non-primitive data type**: String, Date, any class object

So Whenever a method returns something (some value), you must specify what type of value it is returning
E.g.
int getMyData() → this method returns the int type of value

1. Whenever a method returns some value, **the last line of the method** must be returned, followed by the value or variable (of the same type that the method is willing to return)

For example

```
int getMyData()
{
     int a =33;
     return 10; or return a;
}
```

1. Whenever a method returns a value, it holds the value that it returns.

The return type can be

- **Primitive data type**: int, float, char, double, boolean
- **Array** → Single dimensional / 2 dimensional
- **Non-primitive data type**: String, Date, any class object

To understand all different return types, consider the below program.

```
public class ReturningValue {

  int getMyData()
  {
    int x =98;

    return  x;
    // return  10;
  }

  String getMyString()
  {
    String s = "my string";

    return  s;
  }
```

```java
int[] getMyArray()
{
   int[] a = {23,54,12,45,78};

   return  a;
}

String[][] getMyTwoDArray()
{
   String[][] str = {

           {"abc1","pqr1","xyz1"},
           {"abc2","pqr2","xyz2"},
           {"abc3","pqr3","xyz3"},
           {"abc4","pqr4","xyz4"}
   };

   return str;
}


public static void main(String[] args) {

   int number = 78;
   System.out.println(number);
   int y  = number;

   ReturningValue ob = new ReturningValue();
   ob.getMyData();
               // it holds the value that it returns

   System.out.println(ob.getMyData());
   int ab = ob.getMyData();
   System.out.println("ab="+ab);

   System.out.println(ob.getMyString());
   String ss = ob.getMyString();
   System.out.println("ss="+ss);
```

```java
int[] xx = ob.getMyArray();

for(int i=0; i<xx.length ;i++)
    System.out.println(xx[i]);


String[][] s = ob.getMyTwoDArray();

for (int i=0;i<s.length;i++)
{
    for (int j=0;j<s[0].length;j++)
    {
        System.out.print(s[i][j]+" ");
    }
    System.out.println();
}

System.out.println(s[0][1]);
  }
}
```

1.11 FINAL AND STATIC KEYWORD

Final can be
1.   **Variable:** we can't change the value of it
consider below example

```java
public class FinalDemo {
  int speed = 100;
  void change()
  {
     speed =200;
  }

  public static void main(String[] args) {

    FinalDemo ob = new FinalDemo();

    System.out.println(ob.speed);
    ob.change();
    System.out.println(ob.speed);
  }
}
```

In this example, there is a data member speed = 100. There is a
method change() we are changing the value of the variable speed.
When we print the speed value in the main method using the class
object, it will be 100. After calling the method change, it will print as
200. it means we are allowed to change a normal variable,

but if we make the variable final

final int speed = 100;

then there will be an error inside the change method

```
final int speed = 100;
void change()
{
    speed =200;
}
```

Cannot assign a value to final variable 'speed'

Make 'speed' not final   Alt+Shift+Enter   Mor

Error: it can not assign a value to a final variable or make speed not final. The above error proves that we can change a final variable's value.

2. Method: it can't be overridden. We can't create the same name of the method in the child class,

consider below example

```
public class OverridingDemo {

    final void myMethod()
    {
        System.out.println("parent method");
    }
}

class ChildOverring extends  OverridingDemo {

    void myMethod()
    {
        System.out.println("Child method");
    }
```

```java
public static void main(String[] args) {

    ChildOverring ob = new ChildOverring();
    OverridingDemo ov = new ChildOverring();
        ob.myMethod();
    }
 }
```

Above is an example of overriding in that I have made a parent class method (myMethod) final, then you may see below error

'myMethod()' cannot override 'myMethod()' in 'InheritanceDemo.ClassA'; overridden method is final

3. Class:it can't be a subclass. You can't create the child class of it, consider below example

consider below example

```java
public  final class ClassA {
   int x;

   void myMethod()
   {
      System.out.println("Parent method");
   }

 }

class ClassB extends ClassA
{
   int y;

   void myMethod()
   {
      System.out.println("Child method");
   }

   public static void main(String[] args) {

      ClassB ob = new ClassB();
      ob.y = 12;
```

```
        ob.x =45;
      }
   }
}
```

In the above example, I have made the parent class (ClassA) final so that you may see the below error.

```
Cannot inherit from final 'InheritanceDemo.ClassA'

Make 'ClassA' not final   Alt+Shift+Enter     More actions...   Alt+Enter
```

Static keyword

consider below example

```
class Student {

   int rno;
   String name;
   static String college="ITS";
}
```

This class is created for students in some particular college, say "ITC," so each object of this class represents a student.

so let's create three objects to represent three students

```
Student s1 = new Student();
Student s2 = new Student();
Student s3 = new Student();
```

Now we know that when we create an object of the class, we get a memory block allocated for each object. This memory is allocated for each data member of each object memory block. We will get three memory blocks for three students as follows.

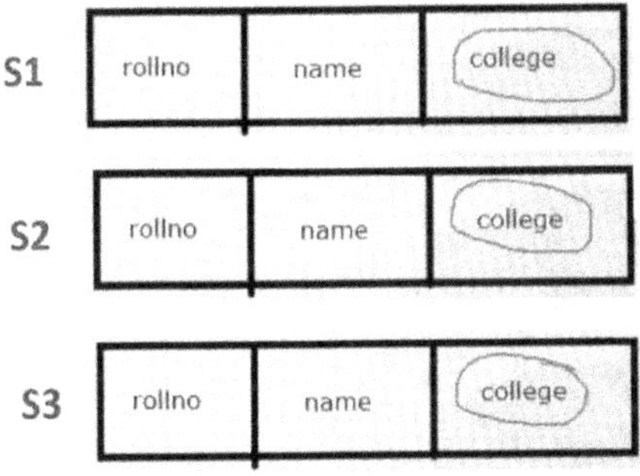

But observe that every student has a common college, so unnecessary three memories are allocated for college name. If there are 500 students, 500 memory blocks will be allocated for storing college names, which is unnecessary.
so we are proposing a static keyword

1. static is used for memory management
2. when you declare a variable as static, it shares a common memory among all the objects

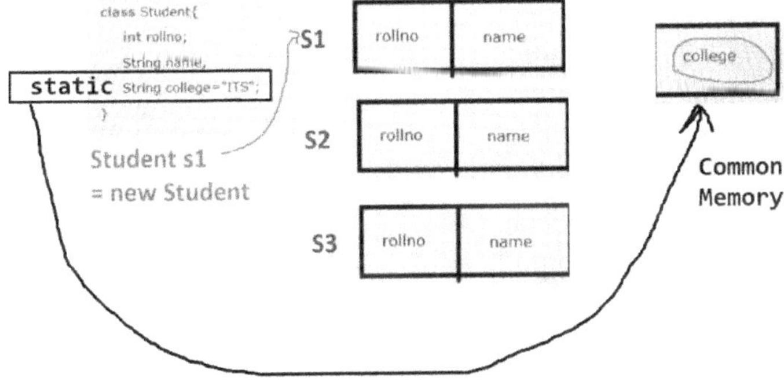

3. any object can access it, and it can change its value as well
4. if any object changes the value of the static variable, then the exact change is reflected for all other objects

See the below example. The student object s2 sets the college name as "ABCD," so all students get the college name as "ABCD" only.

```java
public class Student {

    int rno;
    String name;
    static String college="ITS";

    void display()
    {
        System.out.println("rno="+rno);
        System.out.println("name="+name);
        System.out.println("college="+college);
    }

    public static void main(String[] args) {

        Student s1 = new Student();
        Student s2 = new Student();
        Student s3 = new Student();

        s1.rno=1;
        s1.name="Anand";

        s2.rno=2;
        s2.name="Asha";

        s3.rno=3;
        s3.name="Nilima";

        s2.college = "ABCD";

        s1.display();
        s2.display();
        s3.display();

    }
}
output :
rno=1
name=Anand
college=ABCD
```

rno=2
name=Asha
college=ABCD
rno=3
name=Nilima
college=ABCD

5. Static members can be accessed using class name as well as below

Student.*college* = "XYZ";
System.*out*.println("using class name=" + Student.*college*);

static can be a method as well
below is the syntax of the static method

```java
static void myMethod()
{

}
```

1. Static methods can call (can include) only static members non-static members can not be called inside a static method

Non-static field 'rno' cannot be referenced from a static context

Create field 'rno'   Alt+Shift+Enter   More actions...   Alt+Enter

2.   Vice versa is not true → non-static methods can call static members
3.   The static method can be called using any object or class name
to understand this, consider the below example

```java
public class StaticMethodDemo {
```

```java
int rno;
String name;
public static String college;

void display() // non static method
{
    System.out.println("rno="+rno);// non static member is allowed
    System.out.println("name="+name);
         // non static member is allowed
    System.out.println("college="+college); // static member is allowed
    method2(); // static member is allowed
    method3();// non static member is allowed

}

void method3()
{
    System.out.println("another non static method");
}



public static void method2()
{
    System.out.println("another static method");
}

public static void myMethod() // static method
{
    System.out.println("inside static my method");
    System.out.println(college);// static members are allowed
    // System.out.println(rno); // non static members are not allowed
    // display(); // non static members are not allowed
    method2();// static members are allowed
}

public static void main(String[] args) {

    StaticMethodDemo ob = new StaticMethodDemo();

    ob.method2();
```

StaticMethodDemo.*method2*();
//Static method can be called using class name

```
    }
}
```

4.   You don't need the class name to access static members if we import the class statically.

```
method2();
myMethod();
col
```

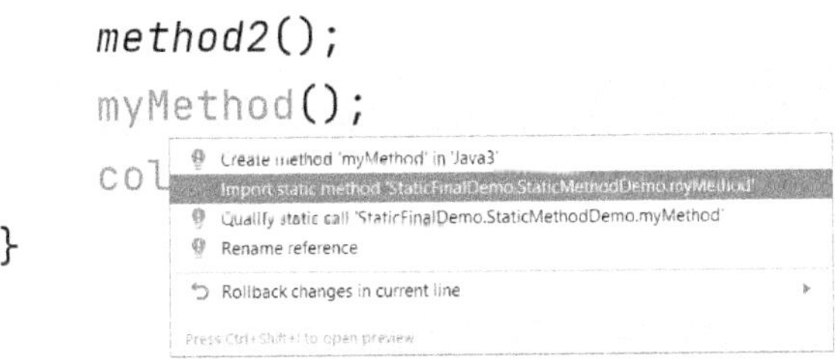


```
}
```

```
import static StaticFinalDemo.StaticMethodDemo.method2;
import static StaticFinalDemo.StaticMethodDemo.myMethod;
import static StaticFinalDemo.StaticMethodDemo.college;
```

Why the main method is static

1. The main method is an entry point of program execution
2. And we don't need to create an object to call this method
3. This method is called automatically when the program is set for execution
4. So internally, in java, the main method is set as static.

1.12 POLYMORPHISM

Polymorphism in Java is a concept by which we can perform a single action in different ways.

Polymorphism is the ability of an object to take on many forms.

There are two types of polymorphism in Java

1. Compile time polymorphism (Static)

2. Runtime polymorphism (Dynamic)

We can perform polymorphism in Java

1. Method overloading

2. Method overriding.

Overloading

Remember, in one class, you can't have more than one identical method, but if you use different parameters for each method, it is possible. Consider the example below.

```
class OverloadingDemo {
  int a ;
  int b;

  void addition()
  {
    int c;
```

```java
      c= a+b;
      System.out.println("c="+c);
   }
void addition(int x)
   {
      int c;
      c= a+x;
      System.out.println("c="+c);
   }

void addition(int x, int y)
   {
      int c;
      c= y+x;
      System.out.println("c="+c);
   }

void addition(double x, double y)
   {
      double c;
      c= y+x;
      System.out.println("c="+c);
   }

void addition(double x, int y, char ch , String s)
   {
      System.out.println("x="+x);
      System.out.println("y="+y);
      System.out.println("ch="+ch);
      System.out.println("s="+s);
   }

public static void main(String[] args) {
      OverloadingDemo ob = new OverloadingDemo();

      ob.addition();
      ob.addition(23);
      ob.addition(23,11);
      ob.addition(1.1,2.2);
      ob.addition(2.2,23,'g',"kjkjk");
```

```
    }
}
```

In the above example, we can see addition is the method defined more than once & it has different arguments. The different arguments can to 2 or more. All arguments can be the same or different.

When you want to call any specific method, then while calling that method, you have to pass the corresponding values of that particular data type.

Overriding

If a subclass (child class) has the same method as declared in the parent class, it is known as method overriding in Java.

consider below example

```java
class OverridingDemo {

    void myMethod()
    {
        System.out.println("parent method");
    }
}

class ChildOverring extends  OverridingDemo {

    void myMethod()
    {
        System.out.println("Child method");
    }

    public static void main(String[] args) {

        ChildOverring ob = new ChildOverring();
        OverridingDemo ov = new ChildOverring();
        // upcasting
```

```
        ob.myMethod();
    ov.myMethod();
  }
}
```

The above example defines myMethod() in the parent class. It is also there in the child class, But the implementation is different. If we create the object of a child class and use that object to call this method, It will give the call to the method in the child class. To call the method in the parent class, you must create a parent class object reference as shown in the program. It is called upcasting.

consider below example:

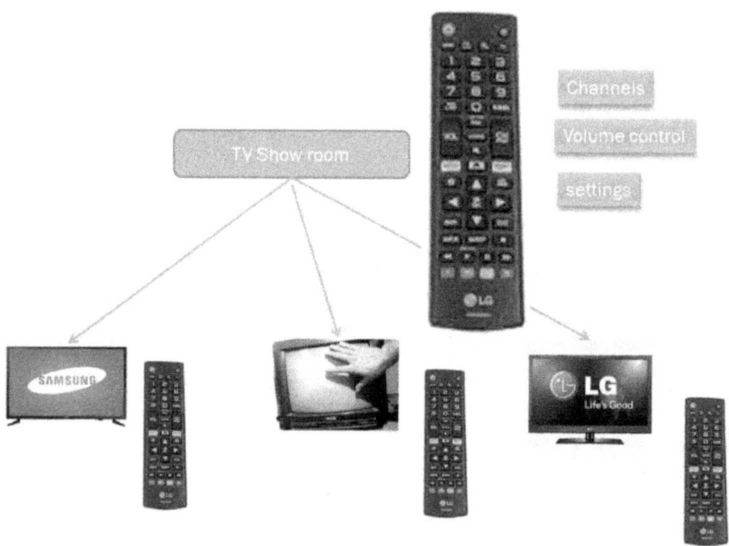

Now assume that you go to a TV showroom and see different TVs belonging to different companies. For example, each TV has it's remote—for example, Samsung, Onida, and LG. If you carefully observe, each remote has certain standard functionality. To change the channels, we have buttons. To change the settings, we have certain buttons, and for volume control, also we have certain buttons. Now almost all of these functionalities are the same. Still, Samsung thought I wanted to implement this functionality in my way, as Onida and an LG also thought. In a TV showroom, the common methods are there for volume control, changing the channel, and changing the settings. Still, the implementation is different in their child classes, Samsung Onida and LG.

1.13 ABSTRACT CLASS AND INTERFACE

Abstraction is a process of hiding the implementation details and showing only functionality to the user.

Another way, it shows only essential things to the user and hides the internal details.

- For example, you are sending SMS where you type the text and send the message. You don't know the internal processing of the message delivery.

There are two ways to achieve abstraction in java

using the Abstract class. We can achieve 0 to 100% abstraction while using Interface. We can achieve 100% abstraction

1. **Abstract class :**
- We must declare an abstract class with an abstract keyword.
- It can have abstract and non-abstract methods.
- It cannot be instantiated. We can't create the object of abstract class
- It can have constructors and static methods also.
- It can have final methods that will force the subclass not to change the method's body.
- abstract class A{}
- abstract void printStatus();//no method body and abstract
- The inherited class of abstract class must implement all the abstract methods
- If it does not implement all or some methods, then it must be declared as abstract

Let us understand this with the help of an example.

```java
abstract class AbstractclassDemo {

    abstract void run(); // abstract  - declared
    abstract  void start();

    void myMethod() // non abstract method - defined
    {
        System.out.println("myMethod");
    }

}

class ChildAbstract extends AbstractclassDemo
{
    void run()
    {
        System.out.println("run");
    }

    void start()
    {
        System.out.println("start");
    }

    public static void main(String[] args) {

        AbstractclassDemo ob = new ChildAbstract();

        ob.run();
        ob.start();
        ob.myMethod();

    }

}
```

In the above example, run() and start() are the abstract methods. They are just declared we don't have a body for it, and a Keyword abstract is written before the these methods

mymethod() is a non-abstract method because it has the body

The child class ChildAbstract is inheriting the parent class AbstractClassDemo. When we set the parent class to the child class, there is a compulsion to implement the abstract methods. Here those are run and start if we don't implement these two methods in the child class, then it will show us an error and ask us to implement them. Otherwise, you need to declare this child's class as abstract.

Interface :

The Interface is almost like an abstract class, but all its methods are abstract. the Interface is created as below

```
interface interfaceName
{
}
```

and the methods are written as below

```
interface interfaceName
{
        void run();
        void start();
}
```

Here we don't have to mention the abstract keyword. By default, the methods in the Interface are public and abstract,

you can have static concrete methods. also, the access modifier for the static method will be public

we can also have a default concrete methods methods

concrete methods mean non-abstract methods

To implement these methods, we have to create a child class. Now to make Interface as a parent of this child class, we have to use a keyword implement, not 'extends' as in class inheritance.

- The implemented method must be public.
- (as during overriding a method, you can not decrease the scope of access specifiers)
- We must implement all methods in the child class, or the class should be declared abstract if it doesn't implement all methods.

for example

```java
public interface InterfaceDemo {

    void start();
    void run();

    default void display()
    {
        System.out.println("display");
    }

    static void method1()
    {
        System.out.println("display");
    }

}

class  ChildInterface implements  InterfaceDemo
{
    public void run()
    {
        System.out.println("run");
    }

    public void start()
    {
        System.out.println("start");
```

```java
        }

        public static void main(String[] args) {

            InterfaceDemo ob = new ChildInterface();
            ob.start();
            ob.run();
            ob.display();
            // ob.method1();// not allowed
            InterfaceDemo.method1();
            // for static members

        }

    }
```

Using Interface, we can implement multiple inheritances. How, let's see that,

We know that to implement multiple inheritances, we have an issue of ambiguity. If the same name or method is there in 2 different classes, then which method to call by the child class object is the ambiguity.

now consider the below example

```java
public interface AnotherInterface {

    void start();
    void run();

    void display();
}

interface Interface2
{
    void display();
}

class ChildInterface2 implements AnotherInterface,Interface2
```

```java
{
  public void run()
  {
    System.out.println("run");
  }

  public void start()
  {
    System.out.println("start");
  }

  public  void display()
  {
    System.out.println("display");
  }

  public static void main(String[] args) {
    ChildInterface2 ob = new ChildInterface2();
    ob.display();

    AnotherInterface ob1 =  new ChildInterface2();
    ob1.display();

    Interface2 ob2 =  new ChildInterface2();
    ob2.display();
  }

}
```

In the above example, we have two interfaces, a parent class, and one child class. In both the interfaces, we have the method display(). But because this is an interface, the implementation of this display() method is not there in the Interface. Its actual implementation will be there in the child class even if we create the object of the child class. Or the parent interface's reference and give a call to the display method. There is no question of which display method is to be called. the actual implementation of the display method is only going to be called, so in this way, there is no question of ambiguity, and hence we can very comfortably implement the multiple inheritances using interfaces

1.14 EXCEPTION HANDLING

Exception : Exception is the unplanned event that can cause the trouble.

Above is the general definition of the exception

in programming it is the unexpected event that occurs during the execution of the program

Consider below programs

Program 1 :

```
public class DivisionDemo {

public static void main(String[] args) {

int a = 10;

int b = 2;

int c = 0;

c = a / b ;

System.out.println("c="+c);

System.out.println("end of the program");

}

}
```

In the above program, there is a division operation. We have the divisor, and its value is 2. In this case, the program will execute very commonly, and we will get the output without interruption. But suppose if the value of b is zero and if we try to divide any value by zero, we know that the answer will be infinity, which is undefined. Now, if you run the program, the program will execute till the line where C is equal to a / b is written. After that, the control will break. And no further statements will get executed.

Program 2 :

```java
public class ArrayDemo {

public static void main(String[] args) {

int[] a = new int[5];

a[0] = 10;

a[1] = 13;

a[2] = 20;

a[3] = 11;

a[4] = 50;

a[5] = 111;

for (int i=0;i<a.length;i++)

System.out.println(a[i]);

System.out.println("end of the program");

}

}
```

In the above program, we have defined the array of size five. We know that the indexing of the array starts from 0. Here you can see the values that have been added are till the 5th index. But since the array size is five, the last index of the element must be 4. Here we are trying to access the 5th index location of the array and putting the value in it. So the program till index four will work without any issue, the moment it tries to access the 5th location program will lose its control, and no further treatment will get executed.

in these two programs, the point from where the control of the program has broken, we have a few more statements after that, and they don't have any problems or issues in them, so because of this issue, further statements are not going to execute
In the statement from which the program control has broken, we say that the Exception has occurred, and to make the further statements to execute and not to break the program's control, we have to handle this Exception and the process of doing this is exception handling.

exception handling can be done using two ways
1. try-catch block
2. throws keyword

Try catch block is used surrounded with the suspected statement where you think there can be an exception for example

```java
public class DivisionDemo {

public static void main(String[] args) {

int a = 10;

int b = 1;

int c = 0;

try {

c = a / b ;

}

catch (Exception e)

{
```

```
System.out.println("inside catch block");

}

System.out.println("c="+c);

System.out.println("end of the program");

}

}
```

In the above program, if The control comes at the line c=a/b, And here b is zero, we know that anything divided by zero is infinity. The control is about to break, but it will not come out of the program directly. It will go to the catch block, and the further statements will execute.

You can print other information about the Exception using object 'e.'

System.out.println(e.getMessage()); →This will print the exception message

System.out.println(e.getClass()); → this will print the exception class

e.printStackTrace(); → this will print the complete stack trace of the the exception

this we have to add inside the catch block as below

```
catch (Exception e)

{

System.out.println(e.getMessage());

System.out.println(e.getClass());

e.printStackTrace();
```

```
}
```

the output will be as follows

/ by zero

class java.lang.ArithmeticException

c=0

end of the program

java.lang.ArithmeticException: / by zero

at ExceptionHandling.Division.main(Division.java:10)

Throws : Throws does not handle the exception it only informed the method that there would be an exception inside the method.

for example

```java
public class ReadFile {

public static void main(String[] args) throws FileNotFoundException

{

FileInputStream fis = new FileInputStream("D:\\amol.txt");

}

}
```

In the above example, we are trying to read a file at D drive amol.txt. Now, the file input stream takes a string as an argument. There is no way to check whether the string is incorrect path format, so if the path is not in the correct format, there would be a problem, so we have to inform the method that if the path is not right, there would be an exception FileNotFoundException.

throw keyword : This keyword is used to throw a user-defined Exception with a custom message. Whenever in your program, there is a situation where you forcefully want to stop the execution, and you don't want the further statement to be executed. In this case, we can use the throw keyword. Below is the example

```java
public class NumberDemo {

public void checkNumber(int i)

{

if(i<=10 && i>=1)

System.out.println("We are safe");

else

throw new ArithmeticException("we are in danger");

}

public static void main(String[] args) {

int a = 11;

System.out.println("checking numbers");

NumberDemo ob = new NumberDemo();

ob.checkNumber(a);

System.out.println("end of the program");

}

}
```

In the above program, we are checking whether the number is between 1 to 10 or not. If the number is between 1 to 10, then we will print we are safe, and it will print all the further statements. If the number is not between 1 and 10, it should not execute the last statement after checking the number, and there it will throw the Exception with the custom message "we are in danger."

The Exception is a parent class of the throwable, and the throwable is the child class of object who is the superclass of all the classes. If you want to see the Exception class hierarchy, you can search for java docs on Google, and you will get all the classes under the Exception.

1.15 WRAPPER CLASS

We frequently use some data types like int, float, double, char, boolean

int - can hold whole numbers
float, double - can have decimal numbers
char - can have a single character
boolean - can hold 'true' or 'false' values

These data types are known as primitive data types. Their job is to hold the data.

Java is an object-oriented programming language. It sometimes requires objects rather than variables. For example, in the next chapter, we will learn about collections, in that various classes hold the collection of elements. Java array also has collections of elements. Still, in the case of Array, it can keep only similar types of elements. The collection can hold different types of data (heterogeneous elements). Sometimes we may need to make any collection variable that would accept only a particular kind of element. For example, strings integers it selects understand this with the help of an example.

```
ArrayList al = new ArrayList();
al.add("a1");
al.add("a2");
al.add("a1");
al.add(23);
```

```
al.add(2.8);
al.add('j');
```

Now, this ArrayList 'al' can accept all types of values, and it will create the list. Still, if we want to restrict this list with any particular element, We can do it as below.

```
ArrayList<String> al = new ArrayList<>();
```

```
al.add("a1");
al.add("a2");
al.add("a1");
al.add(23); // error
```

now, if I want to accept integers only then can I write a code as below

```
ArrayList<int> al = new ArrayList<>();
```

We can not mention anything other than class inside the angled brackets.

So here, the wrapper class comes into the picture; for every primitive data type, there is an equivalent wrapper class available in Java.

Primitive Type	Wrapper class
boolean	Boolean
char	Character
byte	Byte
short	Short
int	Integer
long	Long

float	Float
double	Double

Now, if we have a primitive data type, for example, int, and if you want to convert it into non-primitive, we can convert it as below.

int i =5; // primitive data type

Integer ii = new Integer(5); // wrapper class
Integer ii = new Integer(i); // wrapper class

The above process is known as boxing or wrapping
we can directly also a sin the primitive data types value to non-primitive data type variable as below

Integer value⁻ i;
Integer value= 5;
This is known as autoboxing for auto wrapping

We can do the reverse way as well means if we have a non-primitive data type, we can convert it into a primitive data type as well,

for example

Integer ii = new Integer();

int i = ii.intValue();

It is known as unboxing or unwrapping.

we can do the same as below

int i = ii ; this is known as autoboxing or auto unwrapping

Converting from string

The other importance of the wrapper class is we can convert primitive values stored in the form of strings into their Type, for example.

String str = "11";

 Now, this 11 is an integer value. Stored into string variable now, this will be considered as spring only, but if you want to use it as an integer, then you have to convert it as below.

int i = Integer.parseInt(str);

Here was the method defined inside the class integer, and of course, it is a static method because it is called using its class name.

 Similarly, we can convert The Other types of values as well, for example.

Double & float value conversion :
String s3 = "56.5";
double d1 = Double.*parseDouble*(s3);
float f1 = Float.*parseFloat*(s3);

Boolean value Conversion

String str = "false";
boolean b = Boolean.*parseBoolean*(str);

if(b)
    System.*out*.println("this is true");
else
    System.*out*.println("this is false");

We can almost convert all types of primitive data types that are stored in the string into their Type. Accept the character for converting the character if it is stored in the form of the string. We cannot convert it as above. However, we have specific ways with the help of which we can convert a character stored in the form of a string, and one of the ways is shown below.

```
String s6 = "d";
char c = s6.charAt(0);
```

1.16 SQL

SQL - Structured Query language is used for database management systems.

Earlier, we used to maintain the data in notebook registers; later, we started to hold it in the files. but even the files in the computer had some limitations in data maintenance like

1. redundancy (deal with duplicate data)
2. deal with related data

We can deal with the above two challenges using a database management system.

We have a language, SQL, to implement the DBMS (database management system). We can implement this language in different softwares like MySQL, Oracle, MongoDB, etc.

We will learn SQL by referring to MySql. See, the queries are almost the same, and it doesn't matter if you implement it in Mysql, Oracle, or any other DB software.

So first, download and install MySql from its official website. It is available for all operating systems like Windows/Mac or Linux.

let's say you have downloaded and installed it on windows
open the command prompt, type the password, and enter

Below are some essential commands in SQL that you can try on the MySQL command prompt.

- Create database : Create database dbName;
- Show databases; --: it shows all the databases present in the SQL
- Select database : use dbName;
- Show tables;:-- > it displays all the tables in the database.
- Create table : - create table tblName(varName1 datatype, varName2 datatype, varName3 datatype, varName4 datatype, varName5 datatype,.....);

int a; → data type variable → java variable declaration

Data types in SQL

int → int
String → varchar(size)

Let's create a table student with column → id, name, branch, marks

- Add a record in a table: -
insert into tblname values(val1,val2,...);

- To see the records in a table
Select * from student;

To retrieve specific records, The 'where clause' is used.

Select * from student where colName = value;
- Find the record of a student whose id =1
- Find the record of a student whose name=' ritesh'
- Find the records of a student whose marks are less than 60

- Find the records of a student whose marks are greater than 60

Note :

If it is an int - write the value as it is

If it is varchar - write the value in a single quote.

8. Update command
- update student set name='abhijit' where id =4;
- Update tblname set col=val, col2=val,col3=value where condition.

Never use where clause the updating column value itself, but it works.

Like operator

- Find all the records of students whose name starts with 'a'
- Select * from student where name like 'a%'
- Find all the records of students whose name ends with 't'
- Select * from student where name like '%t'
- Find all the records of students whose name contains 'i'
- Select * from student where name like '%i%'
- Select * from student where name like '%it%'

When I say - select * from tblName

* mean all the columns in the table
- You can specify the column if you require any specific.
- select id,name from tblName;

For example

```
mysql> select id,name from student;
+-------+----------+
| id    | name     |
+-------+----------+
|    1  | abhijit  |
|    2  | ritesh   |
|    3  | sonali   |
```

```
|   4 | abhijit |
|   5 | Amol    |
+------+---------+
```

Below is the command if you want to specify some other display name to some column

```
mysql> select id as rollNo,name from student;
+--------+---------+
| rollNo | name    |
+--------+---------+
|      1 | abhijit |
|      2 | ritesh  |
|      3 | sonali  |
|      4 | abhijit |
|      5 | Amol    |
+--------+---------+
```

Desc tblName: it describes the table structure, with column names & their type

- Create → DDL
- Select → DDL
- Insert → DML
- Update → DML
- Delete → DML

1. DDL - data definition language queries
2. DML - Data Manipulation language queries

What is difference between

Delete, truncate , drop

Drop	Delete / truncate

1. Drop command is used in context with
   a. Database
   b. Tables
E.g.
Drop database dbName;
Drop table tblName;
	1. Delete / truncate are used in context with tables only
	E.g.
	a. Truncate tblName;
	b. Delete from tblName;

Drop command destroys your database or table.	• It deletes (both commands) records in the table only • It doesn't delete /destroy the table structure
	Delete: can be written with the where clause so that a specific record can be deleted (if you don't use the where clause, it will delete all the records) **Truncate:** it can't be written with a where clause here. All the records are deleted.

1.17 JDBC

JDBC - Java Database connectivity
It is a bridge between Java and the database. It is used to fire the queries from Java code on SQL. Now to implement this, there are four simple steps.

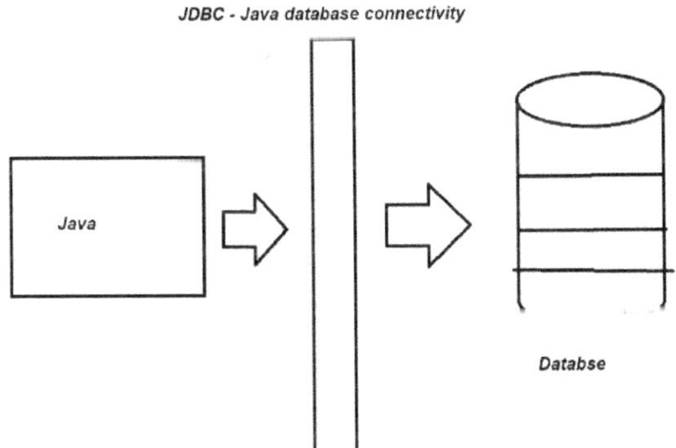

1. loading a driver
2. creating a connection
3. creating a statement
4. executing a query

Now let's see how to code these four steps. Understand one thing as I said that I am going to implement the JDBC by considering my SQL. We can implement the same for any other database like Oracle MongoDB and any other database. Only two things will change the connection string & the classpath.

1. **Loading a driver** (https://dev.mysql.com/downloads/connector/j/)

First, download the MySQL connector from the above link (if you are using any other database like Oracle or MsSql, then you have to download its corresponding SQL connector. You will get it on their official website)

 Now add this connector to your library. Below are the steps if you want to set the library with this connector

1. Intellij Idea steps
- Create a lib folder in your java project
- Copy this connector JAR file in that folder
- right-click on your project → open the module setting
- Click on libraries
- Click on the plus icon at the top
- Click on Java
- Expand your project
- select your lib folder
- say ok
1. Eclipse steps
- Create a lib folder in your java project
- Copy this connector JAR file in that folder
- Right-click on the JAR file
- Click on build path and then click on configure build path

Now you can write the below code to load the driver.

Loading a driver
Class.*forName*("com.mysql.cj.jdbc.Driver");

2. Creating a connection : While creating a connection, you have to establish the connection between my SQL and Java, so take the username and password in one string and maintain one more String for the connection URL as below

String user = "root";

```
String pass = "root";
String url = "jdbc:mysql://localhost:3306/dbName";
```

once you have this you can create the connection using below statement

```
Connection con = DriverManager.getConnection(url,user,pass);
```

3. Creating a statement : Create a statement using the below code here. The con is the object created in the above step

```
Statement st = con.createStatement();
```

4. executing a query

We can categorize the queries as below
Insert, update, delete, select
DML   data manipulation language (Insert, update, delete)
DDL - Data Definition Language (select)

First, we'll see how to deal with DML queries. The code is as below.

```
String sql ="delete from student where rno=10";
st.executeUpdate(sql);
```

You can write any DML query (insert, update, delete) and execute it here.

The code is how to execute the DDL query that is selected below. Now, understand one thing: the queries that were fired, for example, insert update delete; we don't see anything as an output on the console. Still, when you hit the select query, we see the output on the console. We see the records retrieved now. We have to print it if you run this in a Java Program. the code is as below

```
String sql ="select * from student";
ResultSet rs = st.executeQuery(sql);

while(rs.next())
{
  System.out.print(rs.getInt("rno")+" ");
  System.out.print(rs.getString("name")+" ");
  System.out.print(rs.getString("branch")+" ");
```

```java
        System.out.println(rs.getInt("marks"));
}
```

1.18 COLLECTIONS

Collections are yet another essential topic from Java. As the name suggests, it must have a collection of different elements. Still, when I say that, I remember I already have one concept called Arrays in Java.

The problem with arrays is that we can store only similar types of elements, and arrays are fixed in size.

In collections, they have a growable nature and can store heterogeneous elements. When I say collections are growable, we can increase or decrease the collection size. But at what cost. Consider below example

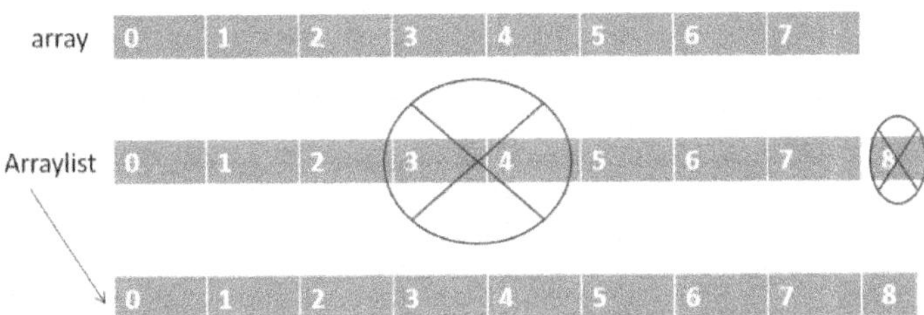

Suppose I have an ArrayList, one of the collection classes. It has size 8. Initially, elements are stored from 0 to 7. let's say I want to store one more value. For that, I need one more place. Now it won't happen that We will create one new place and add new value to it. It will create an entirely new list with one extra place. It will add these newly added elements to it, then point the previous list to this new list, and We will discard the previous list.

Hence we can say that arrays are suitable if we know the size in advance.

Let's quickly see the difference between arrays and collections.

Arrays	collections
Arrays are fixed in size	collections are growable in nature
With respect to memory arrays are not recommended to use	With respect to memory collections recommended to use
With respect to performance arrays are good	with respect to performance collections are not recommended
Arrays can hold only homogeneous type of data	Collections can hold homogeneous as well as heterogeneous type of data
Arrays can hold both primitive and non primitive type of data	collection can hold only non primitive type of data

Below is the structural hierarchy of collection and its child classes

The collection is an interface; it has three child interface lists, queue, and set, and each interface has its child classes. Understand that a collection is a parent class, so whatever methods we already have in collections are equally applicable in all child classes. It's just that Due to specific properties, a little bit of difference will be there.

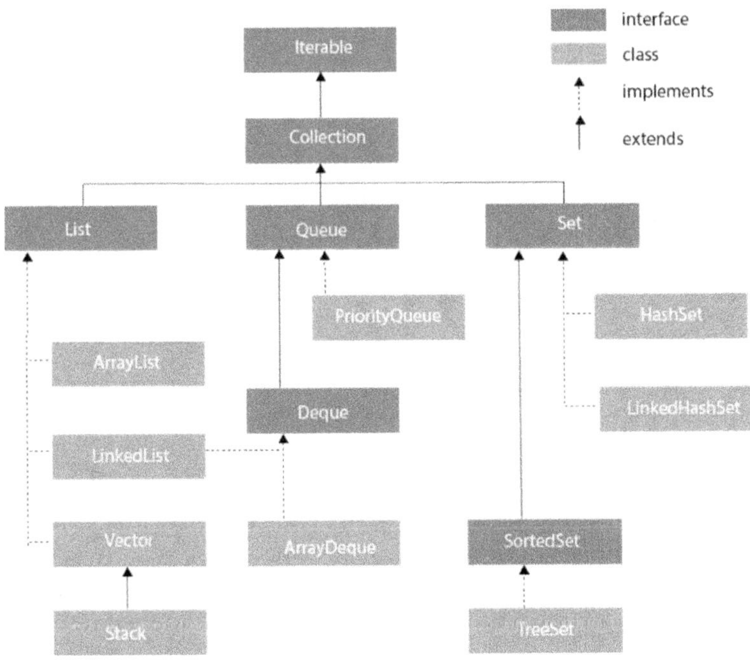

So what we are going to do is we will learn the first type of collection, that is ArrayList, in detail. That is all of the methods we are going to implement. And we will see the new functionalities for the other types of classes, for example, linked list, vector, array DQ, and the other courses. Because the methods that we have already seen in ArrayList are equally applicable here.

1. **List Interface :**

- The list is the child interface of the Collection interface.
- And it inherits a list-type data structure wherein we can store the ordered collection of objects.
- List interface implements classes like ArrayList, LinkedList, Vector , and Stack.
- All of these classes can have duplicate values and heterogeneous elements too.

- Various methods used for the operations like insert, delete, and access the elements from the list are there in the list interface.

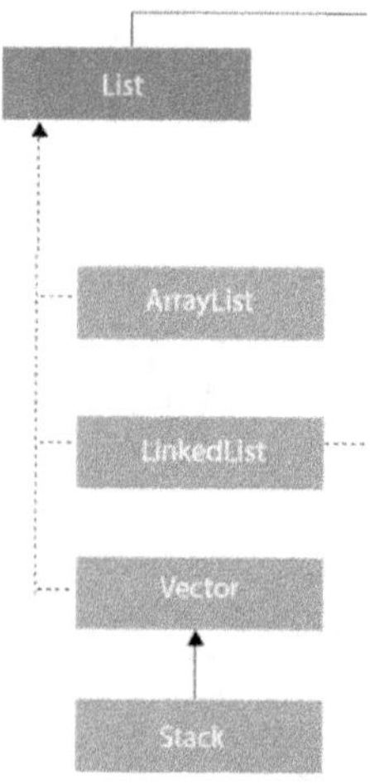

The list has four child classes

1. ArrayList
2. LinkedList
3. Vector
4. stack

Almost all of these classes will have similar methods because these are the child classes of the same interface. Only a little difference will be there among them so let's learn ArrayList first. now in the Array list, we will learn all the functions available, and in the other classes, we will learn the new methods we have because the ways we are going to learn in ArrayList will be equally applicable in the other courses as well

ArrayList :

Let's first learn to create the ArrayList and add a new element. Consider the below program.

```
ArrayList al = new ArrayList();

al.add("amol");
al.add("sudhir");
al.add("anjali");
al.add(12);
al.add(2.2);
al.add(true);
al.add('v');
```

System.*out*.println(al);

In the above program, we have created an ArrayList and added different elements using the add method. Now here you can understand in the Arraylist al, we can add not just the similar type of elements of but also different types of elements. We have added string, integer, double Boolean also character type of value. it means that ArrayList can accept heterogeneous elements

Also, you can just put the variable of ArrayList (here al) and get the list printed.

you can also print the list using for loop as below

for(int i=0;i<al.size();i++)
   System.*out*.println(al.get(i));

Now size() is the method that gives the total number of elements in the Array list. 'get' method is used to get the value from the list at that particular index. Here i is the index just like array ArrayList is also maintained index-wise, and its first element index is zero.

So in the above method, we have covered three methods add, size, and get
 add() - this method adds element to the list
 size() - this method gives the total number of elements present in the list
 get() - this method gives us the element present at that particular index

There are a few more methods in ArrayList. Let's see them.

clear() - This method clears the list; that is, it makes a list empty. This method checks if you are test is empty or not. If it is empty, it returns true if it is not empty, it returns false
remove() - This method removes a particular element from the list. It can take either index or the object to remove as an argument.

removeAll() - This method removes all elements from the list.

If you want to make a list to accept only specific data types, then you can use the following Syntax.

ArrayList<String> al = new ArrayList<>();
This particular array list will accept only strings.

Consider below example it explains addAll() method in ArrayList

```
public static void main(String[] args) {

  ArrayList<Integer> al1 = new ArrayList<>();

  System.out.println(al1.isEmpty()); // true

  al1.add(89);
  al1.add(77);
  al1.add(66);
  al1.add(67);

  System.out.println("al1="+al1);

  ArrayList<Integer> al2 = new ArrayList<>();

  System.out.println("al2="+al2);

  al2.addAll(al1);

  System.out.println("al2="+al2);

}
```

Output

```
al1=[89, 77, 66, 67]
al2=[]
al2=[89, 77, 66, 67]
```

addAll() method copies elements present in one list into another list

Set() - it sets a particular value at particular index
for e.g.

```
public static void main(String[] args) {

    ArrayList<String> al = new ArrayList<>();

    al.add("amol");     // 0
    al.add("sudhir");   // 1
    al.add("anjali");   // 2
    al.add("satyajeet"); // 3
    al.add("Madhura");  // 4
    al.add("Rahul");    // 5

    System.out.println("al="+al);

    al.set(1,"abc");

    System.out.println("al="+al);

}
```

output :
al=[amol, sudhir, anjali, satyajeet, Madhura, Rahul]
al=[amol, abc, anjali, satyajeet, Madhura, Rahul]

removeIf() - This method helps us remove some elements from the list based on some condition. Its Syntax is as below

removeIf(a -> condition)
Now this 'a' is a variable. You don't need to specify its type. Just identify what type of elements your list holds, and the variable 'a' will acquire the same. Dash followed by angle bracket (->) is called a predicate symbol. After that, you have to put the condition so that based on that particular condition, this method will remove the elements in the list.

for example, if below is the list

```
ArrayList<String> al = new ArrayList<>();

al.add("amol");    // 0
al.add("sudhir");  // 1
al.add("anjali");  // 2
al.add("satyajeet"); // 3
al.add("Madhura"); // 4
al.add("Rahul");   // 5
al.add("Rani");    // 5
al.add("Raju");    // 5
```

Below Statement will remove all the elements whose length is less than 5

```
al.removeIf( str -> ( str.length() <5 ) );
```

Below statement will remove all the elements that ends with 'i'

```
al.removeIf( str -> ( str.endsWith("i")) );
```

Linked List :

In the Java LinkedList class, a doubly-linked list is used to store the elements. And we can add or remove elements from both sides.

fig- doubly linked list

All the properties are the same as ArrayList, and how it is stored internally is different.

linked list Insertion / deletion

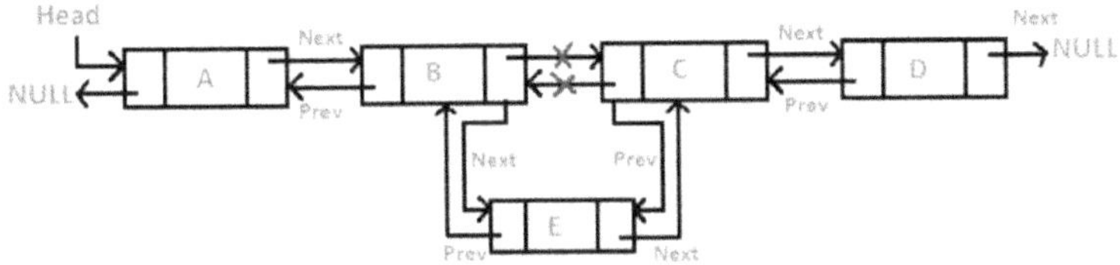

The main advantage of a linked list is that you want to insert any new elements. There is no need to shift it; you must update the pointers next to the previous reference to the above figure.

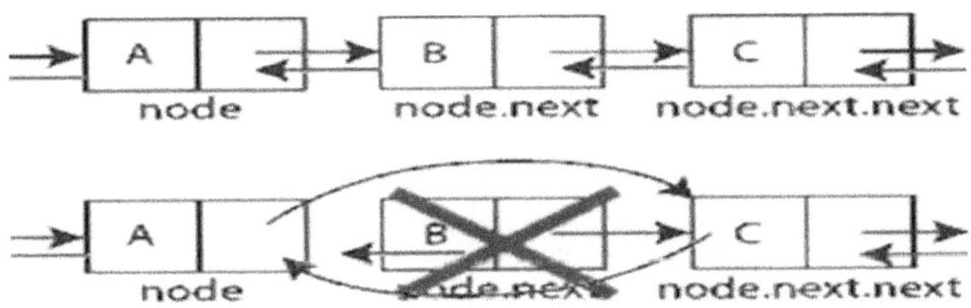

Also, while deleting only the pointers gets updated, No shifting is required.

1. the linked list will be your best choice if you are frequent operations are insertion or deletion
2. but linked list Will Be Your Worst child if you are for frequent operations are retrieval

A linked list has many methods similar to ArrayList, so here we will not implement the same methods because they are equally applicable in a linked list. Here, we will implement only the new methods. The list of the methods which are available in ArrayList as well as in the linked list is below.

add()
addAll()
remove()
removeAll()
removeIf()
clear()

get() & set()
isEmpty()
Collections.sort(list)

New Methods in Linked List are below

addFirst() - This adds elements at first
addLast() - this adds elements at last
removeFirst() - this removes the first element
removeLast() -This removes the last element

Consider below example

```java
public static void main(String[] args) {

    LinkedList<Integer> ll = new LinkedList<>();

    ll.add(23);
    ll.add(13);
    ll.add(26);
    ll.add(73);
    ll.add(20);
    ll.add(33);

    System.out.println(ll);

    ll.addFirst(0);
    ll.addLast(99);
    System.out.println(ll);

    ll.removeFirst();
    ll.removeLast();

    System.out.println(ll);

}
```

Vector

Almost all the properties of the vectors are the same as ArrayList. Only the difference is vectors are thread-safe means synchronized. Now, this thing happens internally in the backend in the front end. When you write a code for vector and its different methods, you don't have to worry about what synchronization and non-synchronization are happening in the backend.

Now let's quickly understand what synchronization and non-synchronization are with the help of the simple example below.

Consider there is a file where suppose five users are going to write. Now consider all users have started writing in that file at a time; This will complete the work quickly. But suppose user 'A' has started writing from one particular point, and let's say user 'B' has also begun writing from some different point. It may happen that user A reached the point where B starts, so this will be an inconsistent state. Hence it is said that the non-synchronized processes are faster, but they are not thread-safe.

On the contrary, consider the same example wherein a file is to be written with the help of 5 users. Still, when one user works, the other users will be locked when the first user completes their work. Then the next user's lock is released, and that user works on it now. This process will take a little bit more time but will be thread-safe.

Now obviously, as we say, vectors are synchronized. That is, their thread-safe, meaning they are slower in process.

Vector is a legacy class.

Now when I say Legacy, what does it mean? Legacy means something that has come from inheritance. Here the vector is Legacy class. When Java was invented, the collection framework was not there. The vector class had done the job of collection. It had specific methods that are still there. At least for now, they are not deprecated. Letter on when the collection framework came, the vector class was re-engineered and is included inside the collection framework. Hence vector class is known as the Legacy class.

Vector increments 100% mean they double the array size if the total number of elements exceeds its capacity.

Let's understand this with the help of an example below.

```java
public class VectorDemo2 {

    public static void main(String[] args) {

        Vector<String> v = new Vector<>();
        // default capacity --> 10

        System.out.println("Capacity="+v.capacity()); // 10
        System.out.println("size="+v.size()); // 0

            v.add("sameer");
            v.add("Amol");
            v.add("Sudhir");
            v.add("Satyajeet");
            v.add("Kishor");
            v.add("Akanksha");
            v.add("Sudhir");
            v.add("Satyajeet");
            v.add("Kishor");
            v.add("Akanksha");
            v.add("Akanksha");

        System.out.println("size="+v.size()); // 10
        System.out.println("Capacity="+v.capacity()); // 10

            System.out.println(v);

    }
}
```

Outpt :
Capacity=10
size=0

size=11
Capacity=20
[sameer, Amol, Sudhir, Satyajeet, Kishor, Akanksha, Sudhir, Satyajeet, Kishor, Akanksha, Akanksha]

Stack

You might have seen several books kept one after the other this is a stack. It has last in first-out format. It means that the book that came last can be removed first, and the book entered at first will be removed later, so first in, last out, or last in, first out; this is nothing but a stack.

The stack is a class. And there are two essential methods of the flags like push and pop; push is used to insert the element in the stack, and pop is used to remove the elements from the stack. Using the pop method, you can remove the top element only.

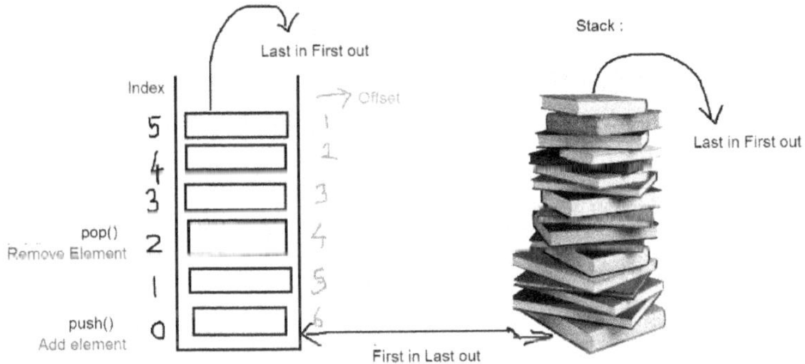

```java
public class StackDemo1 {

    public static void main(String[] args) {

        Stack<String> s = new Stack<>();

        System.out.println(s.empty()); // true

        s.push("Jyoti"); // 0
        s.push("Kishor"); // 1
        s.push("Madhura"); //2
        s.push("Rahul"); //3
        s.push("Sameer"); //4
        s.push("Sri vidya"); //5
        s.push("Amol"); //6

        System.out.println(s.empty()); // false

        System.out.println(s);

        System.out.println(s.pop());
        // removes and returns the top element

        System.out.println(s);

        System.out.println(s.pop());        System.out.println(s);

        System.out.println(s.peek()) ;
        // returns the top element ( does not remove )
        System.out.println(s);

    }
}
```

Output :
true
false
[Jyoti, Kishor, Madhura, Rahul, Sameer, Sri vidya, Amol]

Amol
[Jyoti, Kishor, Madhura, Rahul, Sameer, Sri vidya]
Sri vidya
[Jyoti, Kishor, Madhura, Rahul, Sameer]
Sameer
[Jyoti, Kishor, Madhura, Rahul, Sameer]

Queue

- If you want to represent a group of objects before processing them, we use a queue, e.g., mail sent to a list, SMS ending to a list of numbers.
- Before sending those messages, we have to store the mobile numbers or email ids in a queue. The order in which we added the no. 's or id's in the same order message should be sent.
- Usually, the queue follows the First in, first-out order (In FIFO, the first element is removed first, and the last element is removed at last.) but based on our requirement, and we can implement our priority order as well (priority queue)

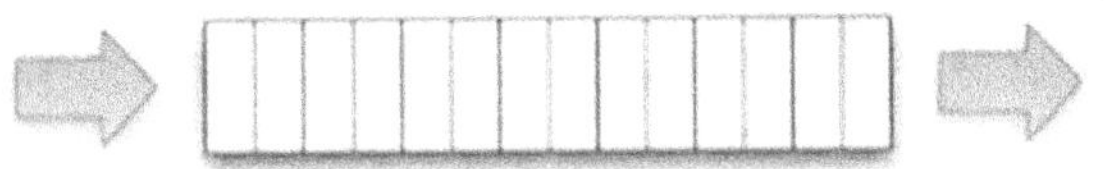

Priority Queue :

- If you want to represent the group of objects before processing based on some priority
- E.g., default natural sorting order or customized sorting order (according to roll no. or according to alphabetical order)
- Insertion order is not preserved. The elements are inserted based on priority.
- Duplicates are not allowed.

- If sorting order is the default natural sorting order, then Heterogeneous elements are not allowed (elements have to be comparable)
- If we are defining our sorting order by comparator interface, then objects need not be homogenous & comparable.
- Null not allowed
- Not thread-safe

Queue Methods

- **offer(object o)** – add an element in the queue
- **poll()** – removes and returns the head element of the queue (if the queue is empty, then it returns null)
- **remove()** – removes and returns the head element of the queue (if the queue is empty, then-No such element exception)
- **peek()** – return head element without removing (if the queue is empty, then returns null)
- **element()** –return head element without removing (if the queue is empty, then-No such element exception)

below is an example of a priority queue


```java
import java.util.PriorityQueue;

public class QueueDemo1 {

  public static void main(String[] args) {

PriorityQueue<Integer> pq = new PriorityQueue<>();

    pq.offer(13);
    pq.offer(23);
    pq.offer(16);
    pq.offer(73);
    pq.offer(10);

    // 10 13 16 23 73
System.out.println(pq);
```

```
    }
}
```

output
[10, 13, 16, 73, 23]

As this is a Priority Queue with the integers ultimately in our output, it should be the numbers in sorted order. Still, looking at the above output, it seems that the result is not in a default natural sorting order.

The reason is that some operating systems do not support priority queues. Sometimes, we may not see the properly sorted output, but internally it is sorted. you can verify it with the below program

```java
import java.util.PriorityQueue;

public class QueueDemo1 {

    public static void main(String[] args) {

        PriorityQueue<Integer> pq = new PriorityQueue<>();

        pq.offer(13);
        pq.offer(23);
        pq.offer(16);
        pq.offer(73);
        pq.offer(10);

        // 10 13 16 23 73
        System.out.println(pq);

        System.out.println(pq.poll());
        System.out.println(pq.poll());
        System.out.println(pq.poll());
        System.out.println(pq.poll());
        System.out.println(pq.poll());

    }
```

```
}
```

output :
```
[10, 13, 16, 73, 23]
10
13
16
23
73
```

ArrayDequeue :

ArrayDeque has the below features

- we can add or remove elements from both sides.
- Null elements are not allowed in the ArrayDeque.
- ArrayDeque is not thread-safe in the absence of external synchronization.
- ArrayDeque has no capacity restrictions.
- ArrayDeque is faster than LinkedList and Stack.

to understand these properties, let's see the below example

```java
public class QueueDemo2 {

    public static void main(String[] args) {

        ArrayDeque<Integer> adq = new ArrayDeque<>();

        adq.offer(13);
        adq.offer(23);
        adq.offer(16);
        adq.offer(73);
        adq.offer(10);

        System.out.println(adq);

        adq.offerFirst(0);
        adq.offerLast(100);
```

```
    System.out.println(adq);

    adq.pollFirst();
    adq.pollLast();

    System.out.println(adq);
  }
}
```

output :
[13, 23, 16, 73, 10]
[0, 13, 23, 16, 73, 10, 100]
[13, 23, 16, 73, 10]

Set

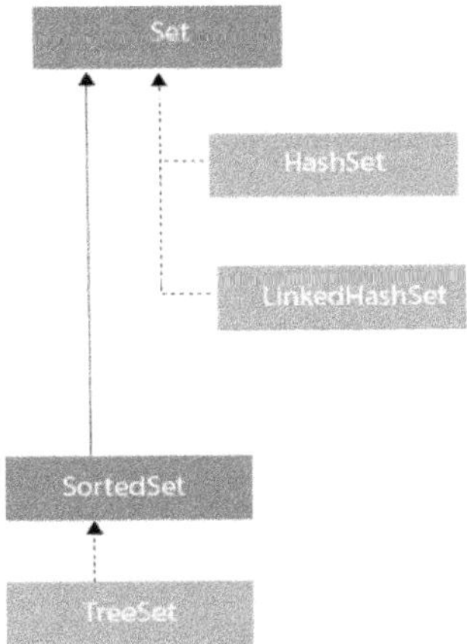

Set is a child class of a collection that does not have any new methods. It uses all the methods from the collection framework only. If you want to represent a group of elements where no duplicates are allowed and insertion order is not preserved, then we use set. set has three main child classes HashSet linked hash set and tree set

1.   HashSet :

In HashSet, duplicates are not allowed. Suppose we are trying to add a duplicate. In that case, we don't get an error or runtime exception. The add() method returns false for duplicates and won't add objects. Insertion order is not preserved

for example


```
public class SetDemo1 {


  public static void main(String[] args) {


      HashSet<Integer> hs = new HashSet<>();

      hs.add(89);

      hs.add(19);

      hs.add(81);

      hs.add(29);

      hs.add(83);

      hs.add(39);

      System.out.println( hs.add(39));

      System.out.println(hs);


  }

}
```

outpt :

false

[81, 19, 83, 39, 89, 29]

2. Linked HashSet

The linked hash set is just like the headset. Only the difference is it maintains the order see the below example.

```java
public class SetDemo2 {

  public static void main(String[] args) {

LinkedHashSet<Integer> lhs = new LinkedHashSet<>();

    lhs.add(89);
    lhs.add(19);
    lhs.add(81);
    lhs.add(29);
    lhs.add(83);
    lhs.add(39);

    System.out.println( lhs.add(39));
    System.out.println(lhs);

  }
}
```

outpt :
false
[89, 19, 81, 29, 83, 39]

3. TreeSet : TreeSets are the sorted set and contains unique elements see the below example

```java
public class SetDemo3 {

  public static void main(String[] args) {

    TreeSet<Integer> lhs = new TreeSet<>();
```

```
        lhs.add(89);
        lhs.add(19);
        lhs.add(81);
        lhs.add(29);
        lhs.add(83);
        lhs.add(39);

        System.out.println( lhs.add(39));
        System.out.println(lhs);

    }
}
```

outpt :

false

[19, 29, 39, 81, 83, 89]

MAP

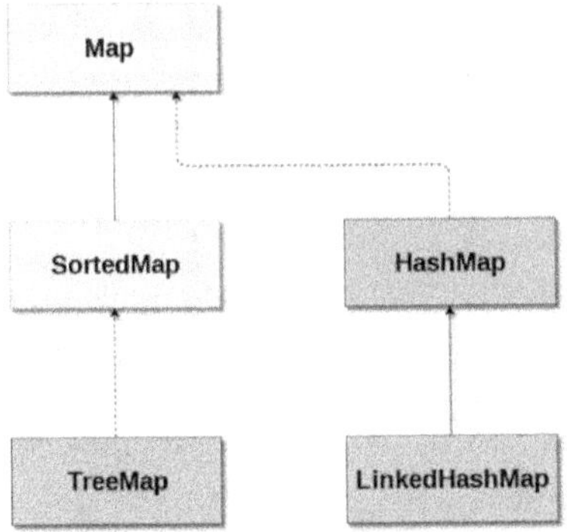

- The map is not a child interface of collections
- If we want to represent a group of objects as key-value pairs, then we should go for a map

Consider below example

Key	Value
101	Amol
102	Rahul
103	Vaishali
104	Ravi

- Both the keys and values are objects only
- Duplicate keys are not allowed
- Values can be duplicated
- Each key-value pair is called an entry. Hence map is considered entry objects
- Duplicate keys are not allowed, but values can be duplicated
- Heterogeneous objects are allowed for both keys and values

- Null is allows for keys(only once) and values any number of times

Map Methods

- Object put(object key,Object value) : to add one key value pair to the map
- If a key is already present then old value will be replaced with new value & returns old value
- m.put(101,"Amol"); → returns null
- m.put(102,"Avi"); → returns null
- m.put(103,"Arnav"); → returns null
- m.put(101,"Ashish"); → returns Amol (old value of 101)
- putAll(map m) → adds all the entries in another map
- m.get(key) → get the value of the key
- m.remove(key) → removes the entry
- m.containsKey(key) → checks the key present in the map or not
- m.containsValue(value)→ checks the value present in the map or not
- m.isEmpty() → checks the map is empty or not
- m.size() → gives the size of the map
- m.clear() → makes map empty
- Set m.keySet() – returns a set of keys
- Collection m.values() – return collection (list) of values
- Set m.entrySet() – returns a set of key value pair

The map has three child classes
1. HashMap
2. LinkedHashMap
3. TreeMap

let's understand them one by one

1. **HashMAP:** This is a collection of key-value pairs with unique keys where insertion order is not preserved.

Example 1: Heterogeneous elements are allowed. Null elements are allowed any number of times for values and only once for keys.

```
import java.util.HashMap;

public class MapDemo1 {

  public static void main(String[] args) {

    HashMap hm = new HashMap();

    hm.put(32,"amol");
    hm.put(71,"sudhir");
    hm.put(78,"madhura");
    hm.put(10,"akanksha");
    hm.put('g',78);
    hm.put(true,7.8);
    hm.put("abcd",7.8);
    hm.put(33,78);
    hm.put(32,78);
    hm.put(11,null);
    hm.put(12,null);
    hm.put(null,23);
    hm.put(null,24);

    System.out.println(hm);

  }
}
```
output:
{32=78, null=24, 33=78, 71=sudhir, g=78, 10=akanksha, 11=null, 12=null, 78=madhura, true=7.8, abcd=7.8}

Example 2 : understanding the method putAll()

```
import java.util.HashMap;
```

```java
public class MapDemo2 {

  public static void main(String[] args) {

    HashMap<Integer,String> hm = new HashMap<>();

    hm.put(32,"amol");
    hm.put(71,"sudhir");
    hm.put(78,"madhura");
    hm.put(10,"akanksha");

    System.out.println("hm="+hm);

    HashMap<Integer,String> hm1 = new HashMap<>();

    System.out.println("hm1="+hm1);

    hm1.putAll(hm);
    System.out.println("hm1="+hm1);


  }
}
```

output :
hm={32=amol, 71=sudhir, 10=akanksha, 78=madhura}
hm1={}
hm1={32=amol, 10=akanksha, 78=madhura, 71=sudhir}

Example 3 : understanding the method isEmpty(), get() , remove() , contains(key) ,contains(value) , size() ,clear().

```java
import java.util.HashMap;

public class MapDemo3 {

  public static void main(String[] args) {

    HashMap<Integer,String> hm = new HashMap<>();
```

```java
        System.out.println("isEmpty="+hm.isEmpty());

        hm.put(32,"amol");
        hm.put(71,"sudhir");
        hm.put(78,"madhura");
        hm.put(10,"akanksha");
        System.out.println("isEmpty="+hm.isEmpty());

        System.out.println("hm="+hm);

        System.out.println( hm.get(71));

        hm.remove(32);
        System.out.println("hm="+hm);

        System.out.println(hm.containsKey(10));
        System.out.println(hm.containsValue("amol"));

        System.out.println(hm.size());

        hm.clear();

        System.out.println("hm="+hm);

    }
}
```

output :
isEmpty=true
isEmpty=false
hm={32=amol, 71=sudhir, 10=akanksha, 78=madhura}
sudhir
hm={71=sudhir, 10=akanksha, 78=madhura}
true
false
3
hm={}

Example 4 : understanding the methods keySet() , valueSet() , entrySet()

```java
import java.util.Collection;
import java.util.HashMap;
import java.util.Set;

public class MapDemo4 {

    public static void main(String[] args) {

        HashMap<Integer,String> hm = new HashMap<>();

        System.out.println("isEmpty="+hm.isEmpty());

        hm.put(32,"amol");
        hm.put(71,"sudhir");
        hm.put(78,"madhura");
        hm.put(10,"akanksha");
        System.out.println("isEmpty="+hm.isEmpty());

        System.out.println("hm="+hm);

        Set s = hm.keySet();

        System.out.println("key set = "+s);

        Collection values = hm.values();
        System.out.println("values = "+values);

        Set entrySet =  hm.entrySet();

        System.out.println("Entry set = "+entrySet);


    }
}
```

output :
isEmpty=true

isEmpty=false
hm={32=amol, 71=sudhir, 10=akanksha, 78=madhura}
key set = [32, 71, 10, 78]
values = [amol, sudhir, akanksha, madhura]
Entry set = [32=amol, 71=sudhir, 10=akanksha, 78=madhura]

2. LinkedHashMAP : This is a collection of key-value pairs unique where insertion order is preserved. let's understand this with the below example (other methods we saw in HashMap are equally applicable here)


```java
import java.util.LinkedHashMap;

public class MapDemo5 {

   public static void main(String[] args) {

LinkedHashMap<Integer,String> lhm
  = new LinkedHashMap<>();

      lhm.put(32,"amol");
      lhm.put(71,"sudhir");
      lhm.put(78,"madhura");
      lhm.put(10,"akanksha");

      System.out.println("hm="+lhm);
   }
}
```

output :
hm={32=amol, 71=sudhir, 78=madhura, 10=akanksha}

3. TreeMAP :   This is a collection of key-value pairs unique where insertion order is a default natural sorting order based on keys. let's understand this with the below example (other methods we saw in HashMap are equally applicable here)

```java
import java.util.TreeMap;

public class MapDemo6 {

    public static void main(String[] args) {

        TreeMap<Integer,String> lhm = new TreeMap<>();

        lhm.put(32,"amol");
        lhm.put(71,"sudhir");
        lhm.put(78,"madhura");
        lhm.put(10,"akanksha");

        System.out.println("hm="+lhm);

    }
}
```

output :
hm={10=akanksha, 32=amol, 71=sudhir, 78=madhura}

Section – 2

Automation with Selenium

2.1 AUTOMATION BASICS

Now we are going to start with automation.

What is automation? Basically, the things we do manually can be done from machines to reduce effort and time. There are many things we used to do manually, but now science has discovered many new gadgets with the help of which we can sit relaxed, and those machines work for us. Below are some examples of manual implementation in traditional ways and automation.

As we can see, all the automation gadgets have drastically reduced human efforts, and it saves time too.

The same applies to Software testing. Suppose all those tests you do manually are done by someone else, and you must monitor them. How does it sound? Great, I guess?

So until now, we have learned that we must test the software before it is released to the customer. Suppose our project is extensive and we need to do regression repeatedly. It means the same set of inputs to each page to verify everything is okay or not, which we need to do after every new change and bug fix. We can do it with automation with the help of several tools.

Examples

Manual implementation in traditional way	Automation
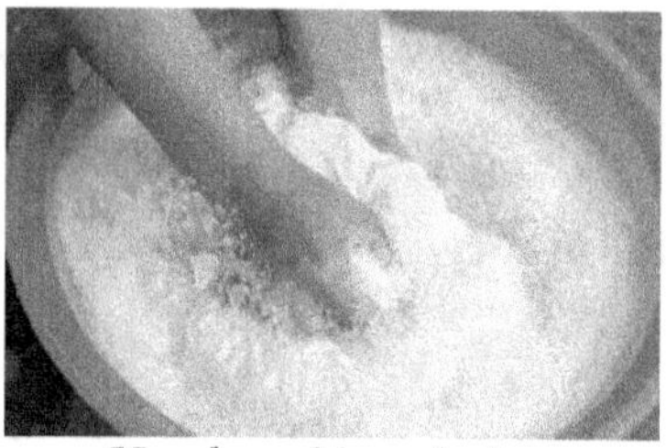 Hand washing clothes	Washing Machine
 Cutting Chopping with hands	 Food Processor

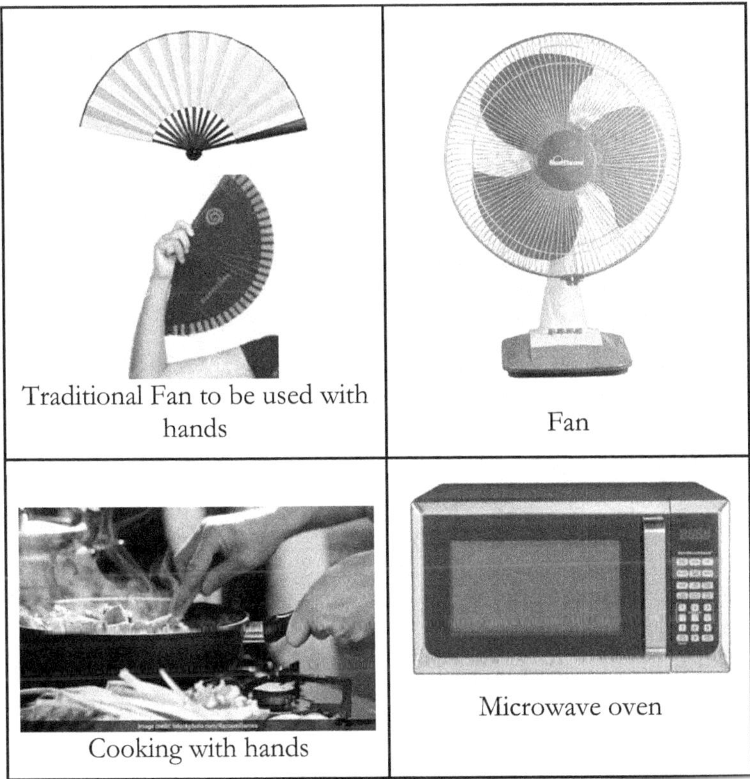

Traditional Fan to be used with hands	Fan
Cooking with hands	Microwave oven

Advantages of automation testing.

1. You can run the tests 24 X 7. You can also start the tests when you leave the office.
2. You don't need a lot of resources; fewer resources can write scripts and automate the tests.
3. All the scripts are reusable. You don't need to write another different script even if the os or browser changes. Automation tests run the same way; you don't need to worry about forgetting something.
4. With the help of automation testing, you find the bugs in the early stages of release.
5. It is more reliable and quicker while running repetitive & standard tests which can't be skipped, which might lead to errors when manually tested.

6. You can test the same tests simultaneously on multiple devices or browsers in less time.
7. We get Automated reports and results.
8. Performance testing that allows more and more users to work simultaneously can be done manually. There are tools available for this type of testing (performance testing). For example, LoadRunner and Jmeter.

Disadvantages of automation testing.
1. It requires more initial developer time for a given feature.
2. It requires a higher skill level of team members
3. Increase tooling needs (test runners, frameworks)
4. It requires complex analysis when a failed test is encountered

Automation testing tools: There are several tools available for automation testing

Jmeter: It is an open source and free tool for performance testing. It is an Apache project that can be used as a load testing tool for analyzing and measuring the performance of various services, with a focus on web applications.

Load Runner: LoadRunner is a software testing tool developed by Micro Focus. It is used for performance testing under load. It can simultaneously simulate thousands of users using the same application software and record and analyze its performance.

UFT: UFT, formerly known as QTP (QuickTest Professional), is an automation testing tool by Micro Focus that implements automated tests to identify bugs in an application under test. The full form of UFT is Unified Functional Testing.QTP was initially developed by Mercury Interactive, which was acquired by Hewlett Packard (HP) in 2006. With version 11.5, QTP was renamed UFT in 2011.

Selenium: Selenium is also an automation testing tool, but it can test web applications only; it can be implemented in java, c#, python, and ruby. Jason Huggins invented Selenium in ThoughtWorks. It is free/open source and widely used in the IT industry to automate tests.

Difference between UFT and Selenium

HP UFT (QTP)	Selenium
It is a licensed tool, and it is expensive.	It's an open-source testing tool; hence it is free.
It is used for testing client-server applications. It can test web-based as well as desktop applications.	Using Selenium, only web applications can be automated.
QTP tests can only be developed in QTP IDE	Selenium can use a wide range of IDEs like Visual Studio, Eclipse, and Net beans.
HP UFT only supports VBScript.	Selenium supports JAVA, .NET, Ruby, Perl, PHP, and many other programming languages.
HP QTP offers excellent technical support.	It has no official support since it is an open source The help we can get from its community forum.
It is more costly to implement	Requires less cost to implement

Why the name Selenium?

As we know, Selenium was invented by Jason Huggins in 2004. At that time, there was a tool called QTP by mercury, and QTP was not a free tool, whereas Jason Huggins invented Selenium which was open source. They both were competitors each other. We know that mercury is an element you might observe in a thermometer or BP checking tool. It is a toxic element. If you take this internally, there is a death threat. However, selenium supplements may save you. So it was a joke by Jason Huggins in an email, "To remove the poison by mercury, we must take selenium supplements." In this way, the name selenium was introduced.

2.2 SELENIUM IMPLEMENTATION AND BASIC METHODS

Till now, we have seen the basic idea of automation. In this chapter, we are going to study the Selenium implementation.

Now, understand Selenium is an Automation Testing tool. When I say it's a tool, you might think I will download some software and install it on my machine. When I install that, it will have specific options with which I will play around, and it will do automation for me. But that's not the case in Selenium. We will create a JAVA project wherein we will write some Java programs and those which, when executed, will do the automation for us.

Understand one more thing Selenium can test web-based applications only. What are web-based applications? Those which open in the web browser. Many well-known web applications are Amazon, Facebook, Gmail, and other online websites. Selenium does not test standalone or desktop applications.

Let's start implementing the Selenium. I hope you are aware of Eclipse or Intellij Idea. These are the Java editors. You can easily search for it on Google and get its setup downloaded and installed. Both are free e an l all the central Idea has paid version, but its Community Edition is free. You can download and install it.

Now how to implement Selenium; we need to create a project in either IntelliJ idea or Eclipse. Now I will show you the steps for creating a project in IntelliJ Idea and completing the project in Eclipse. Letter on I will prefer the IntelliJ idea. But whatever we will learn from now onwards will be equally applicable in Eclipse; it means you can write the same code in Eclipse, and it will work.

first, download the zip file of jars from its official website selenium.dev . go to the download section and download the zip file of jar files related to Java.

Steps to set up selenium project in IntelliJ idea

1. Create a new project in IntelliJ Idea.
2. in that create a new folder a directory
3. Copy all the files inside that extracted zip folder (that you have downloaded from Selenium.dev) and paste them into the lib folder of the IntelliJ idea.
4. Set the lib folder as library (
    Right-click on project -> open module settings → library, click on + icon → java → expand your project → select lib folder → ok.

Steps to set up selenium project in Eclipse

1. create a new JAVA project
2. create a lib folder
3. copy all the jar files into the lib folder.
4. Then select all the jar files
5. right click on it and go to build path, and click on add to build path

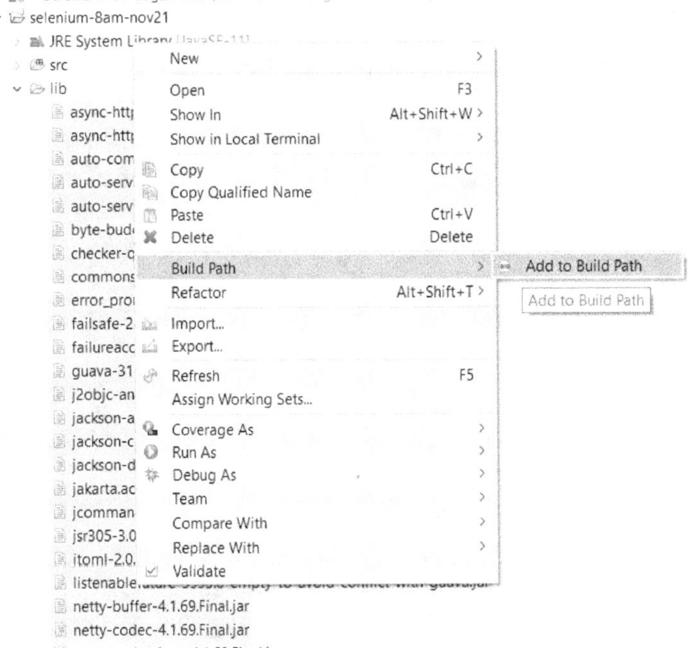

Now there is one more thing left to do. After that will start to write our first Selenium program.

Now you can test only web applications. To test any application, we have to open up the browser.

Earlier in Selenium, the Firefox driver was inbuilt, but the browsers get updated so frequently that every time Selenium needed to upgrade their Jars.

So now we must add a driver file into a project and prefer that driver to open the browser. Let's create one folder in our project and add the corresponding driver.

Now go to the page from where you have downloaded the Selenium jars. Scroll the page a little bit you will see a browser option there. Expand it, and we'll get a list of different browsers from which you have to choose which browser you want to work and download its corresponding driver. The screenshot is given below.

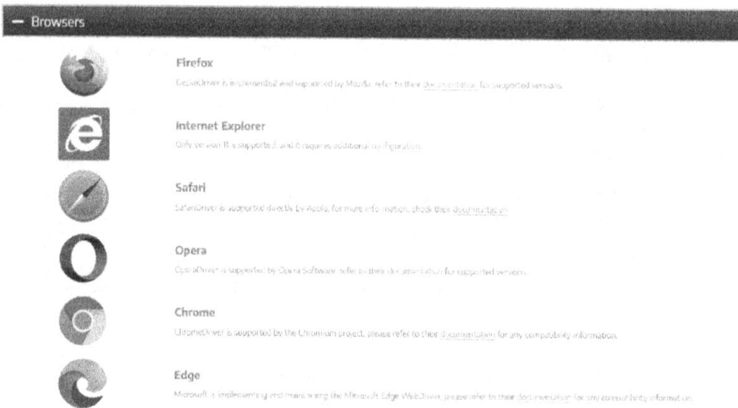

Suppose you want to work with the Chrome browser. Then open the chrome documentation from the same page by clicking on the link documentation, check the version of your chrome and download its corresponding driver.

Create a folder in your project named this as drivers and put this downloaded file into this folder this file will be inside. You must extract that zip file and copy it into your driver folder.

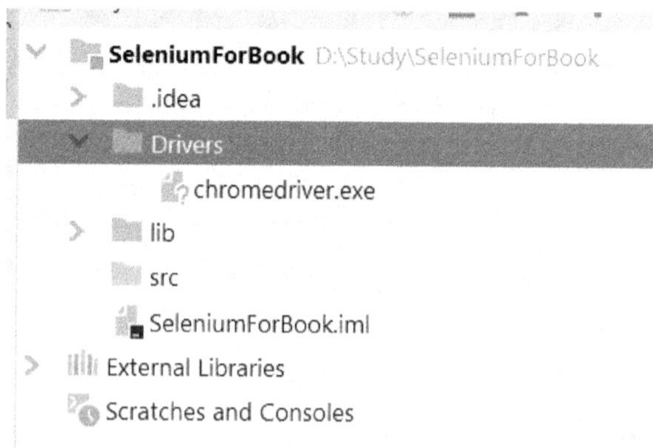

Now let's start writing the first Selenium program to open the browser. Below is the code.

```
import org.openqa.selenium.WebDriver;
import org.openqa.selenium.chrome.ChromeDriver;


public class SeleniumDemo {


  public static void main(String[] args) {

     System.setProperty("webdriver.chrome.driver","path to chrome driver");
     WebDriver driver = new ChromeDriver();
   }
}
```

In the first line of code, which is there inside the main function system.setProperty. setProperty is the method that takes two arguments. The first argument specifies which browser you will work with, and the second parameter specifies the part of your driver. You have to put either the whole part or you can put the later part of your driver, for example

1. Relative path: **Drivers/chromedriver.exe**
2. Absolute   path   :
    D:\Study\SeleniumForBook\Drivers\chromedriver.exe

It is always better to use a relative path. When you run this program, it will open the browser.

This browser will be a completely new instance where you will not observe your saved password, existing extensions, or plugins in your browser. It is just like an incognito window.

The browser is opened, but it is not maximized if you want to maximize the browser, you have to put the following statement that is

driver.manage().window().maximize();

This command will maximize your browser window. If you want to open any website, use the below command.

driver.get("**http://facebook.com**");

You can give any URL into the double quotes, and that particular URL will open in your browser.

We can also get the page title of your webpage using the below method.

driver.getTitle();

If you want to get the correct URL of your webpage, use the below command

driver.getCurrentUrl();

The whole program and its output will look like the below.

```java
import org.openqa.selenium.WebDriver;
import org.openqa.selenium.chrome.ChromeDriver;


public class SeleniumDemo {

   public static void main(String[] args) {


        System.setProperty("webdriver.chrome.driver","Drivers/chrome
driver.exe");
        WebDriver driver = new ChromeDriver();


        driver.manage().window().maximize();


        driver.get("http://facebook.com");


        System.out.println(driver.getTitle());


        System.out.println(driver.getCurrentUrl());


   }
}
```


output :
Facebook – log in or sign up
https://www.facebook.com/

Let's see a few more methods and their uses.

driver.navigate().back();
This command will move back a single step in the web browser's
history.

driver.navigate().forward();
This command will move forward a single step in the web browser's history.

driver.navigate().refresh();
Refresh your web browser.

driver. close(): Close the current window. If there are multiple windows, it will close the current window, which is active, and quit the browser if it's the last window opened currently.
driver.quit(): Quits this driver instance, closing every associated opened window.
e.g., driver.quit();

To understand the close and quit method better, open naukri.com using automation. Along with this website, some popups also open if you use driver.close(), it will only close the current browser window, not the popups. But if you use driver.quit(), it will close not only the current browser but also the popups opened by this browser

Example 1: driver.close();


```
import io.github.bonigarcia.wdm.WebDriverManager;
import org.openqa.selenium.WebDriver;
import org.openqa.selenium.chrome.ChromeDriver;


public class SamplePage {


  public static void main(String[] args) {
```

```
        WebDriverManager.chromedriver().setup();
        WebDriver driver = new ChromeDriver();
        driver.manage().window().maximize();
        driver.get("naukri.com");
        driver.close();
    }
}
```
Example 2 : driver.quit();


```
import io.github.bonigarcia.wdm.WebDriverManager;
import org.openqa.selenium.WebDriver;
import org.openqa.selenium.chrome.ChromeDriver;


public class SamplePage {


    public static void main(String[] args) {
        WebDriverManager.chromedriver().setup();
        WebDriver driver = new ChromeDriver();
        driver.manage().window().maximize();
        driver.get("naukri.com");
        driver.quit();
    }
}
```


WebDriverManager: In about two codes have used a WebdriverManager. It is a class that automatically identifies the version of your browser, and it downloads and stores the driver into your local directory. You don't have to worry about the version of your driver. Also, you don't need to maintain chomedriver.exe (or other browser drivers) in your project. To use this, you have to download the jar files. You will get it quickly on Google. Search for 'webdrivermanager jar download.'

192

2.3 FIND ELEMENT AND FIND ELEMENTS METHODS

In the previous lesson, we learned how to create a Selenium project and some basic Selenium Basic methods for
1. open the browser
2. maximize the browser
3. open the URL
4. finding the page title
5. getting the current URL
6. close and quit

This chapter will explore further; we will automate real and straightforward scenarios. Below is the screenshot of the Login page

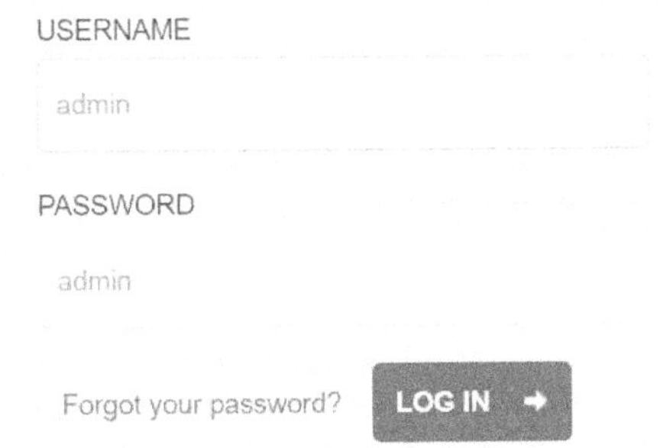

We will open the browser, enter the username and password, and click that login button.
Let's see how to do this.

Now understand one thing, The elements present on the web page we call web elements. To interact with the web elements, we must find them first.

Now to find them, we need to see the HTML code, now don't worry. Even if you don't have any HTML background, follow these steps, and you will be able to find the web element, and you can interact with them at well

1. Right-click on the web page, click on inspect elements, and you will see the HTML code side by the Web page

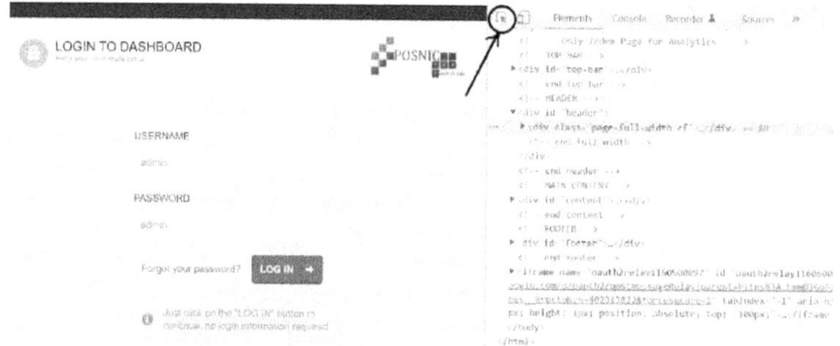

2. Now click on the arrow key at the top. When you click on it, it will turn a blue color, slightly moving your cursor towards the element you want to find.
3. You will observe in the HTML section the code for that particular element will be highlighted; for example, for this username, below is the code.
4. In this code, you will either find the name or id. So You can either use an ID or name to find this web element. Let's see this web element with the help of the code below.

driver.findElement(By.*id*("login-username"));

5. Now we will store this value into a variable of type web element (WebElement is the interface)

```
WebElement txtUsername = driver.findElement(By.id("login-username"));
```

6. If you want to type into this textbox, there is a method, sendKeys, which you can type into as below.

```
txtUsername.sendKeys("admin");
```

- Similarly, you can find the element for the password and type it into it.
- The next element is the button. You can find the button also, but here the operation will not be sentKeys. The operation will be 'click' below is the complete code to automate the login scenario.

```
WebDriverManager.chromedriver().setup();
WebDriver driver = new ChromeDriver();


driver.manage().window().maximize();
driver.get("https://stock.scriptinglogic.net/");


WebElement txtUsername = driver.findElement(By.id("login-username"));
txtUsername.sendKeys("admin");

WebElement txtPassword = driver.findElement(By.id("login-password"));
```

```
txtPassword.sendKeys("admin");
```

```
WebElement btnLogin = driver.findElement(By.name("submit"));
btnLogin.click();
```

FindElements: Find elements returns the list of web elements

To understand this, let's implement one example.
Let's do the same login operation, but this time, we will find the elements by tag name
Earlier, we have seen the locator's ID and name. The tag name is also one of the locators.

```
<input type="text" id="login-username" class="round full-width-input" placeholder="admin" name="username" autofocus="">
```

In the above example, code input is the tag name.

Consider a login page
https://stock.scriptinglogic.net/

We can find the group of elements using tag name input as below
```
driver.findElements(By.tagName("input"));
```

This will return the list of web elements. We can capture it into a list below.

```
List<WebElement> wbList =
driver.findElements(By.tagName("input"));
```

Now, if you want to get every element of this list, you can get it below.

wbList.get(0) → username
wbList.get(1) → password
wbList.get(2) → login button

All three elements are individual web elements. And we can interact with them as below.

wbList.get(0).sendKeys("admin");
wbList.get(1).sendKeys("admin");
wbList.get(2).click();

The complete program is given below

```java
public class FindElementsDemo {

  public static void main(String[] args) {

      WebDriverManager.chromedriver().setup();
      WebDriver driver = new ChromeDriver();

      driver.manage().window().maximize();

      driver.get("https://stock.scriptinglogic.net/");

      List<WebElement> wbList =
driver.findElements(By.tagName("input"));

      wbList.get(0).sendKeys("admin");
      wbList.get(1).sendKeys("admin");
      wbList.get(2).click();

  }
}
```

2.4 DROPDOWNS AND MULTI-SELECT LIST

Now unlike the text box or button, a drop-down is also one of the web elements, and interacting with it is not that straightforward. We have seen that we can find the web element text box, and just by using sendkeys, we can type into it. And for the button also we can find, and we can use the click method and click on it. But to select something from the drop-down, there is a procedure, and we can implement it in 3 simple steps. Those are as below.

1. Find the web element
2. create the object of the select class and pass the web element object into the constructor of it
3. we can select by visible text by value or by index

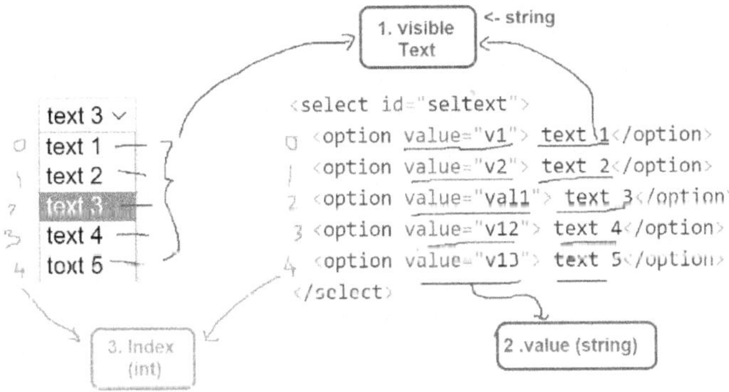

The above diagram shows the drop-down and its corresponding HTML code. The drop-down has some options. Here you can see different options like text one text to text 3. Its HTML code is enclosed between the select flat select tag. We have multiple option tags, which are held with the text visible in the drop-down.

now understand the three terminologies
1. visible text: the text that appears in the drop-down is the text that appears inside the tag option
2. index: if you start numbering all the options in the drop-down beginning with 0, then these numbers are the index
3. Value: in the option tag, there is an attribute value

So we can select an option from the drop-down either by visible text, an index, or value. Let's see how to do that.

- Find the web element.
  WebElement drpSel =
  driver.findElement(By.id("seltext"));

- Create the object of the select class and pass the webelement object into the constructor of it
  Select sel = new Select(drpSel);

- we can select by visible text by value or by index

- By visible text :
  sel.selectByVisibleText("text 3");

- By Index :
  sel.selectByIndex(3); // text 4

- By value :
  sel.selectByValue("v13"); // text 5

Below is the code for the above drop-down

public class DropDownDemo {

```java
public static void main(String[] args) {

    WebDriverManager.chromedriver().setup();
    WebDriver driver = new ChromeDriver();
    driver.manage().window().maximize();
    driver.get("https://amolujagare.com/sample");

    // 1. find the web element
    WebElement drpSel = driver.findElement(By.id("seltext"));

    // 2. create the object of the select class
    Select sel = new Select(drpSel);

    // 3. select the option

    sel.selectByVisibleText("text 3");
    // or
    //sel.selectByIndex(3); // text 4
    //sel.selectByValue("v13"); // text 5
  }
}
}
```

Multi-select list

Multiselect list has almost similar code as that of the drop-down only the difference is there is one attribute
multiple= 'multiple'

Another difference is we can select multiple options at a time.

The procedure to select elements from a multi-select list is almost similar. It is just that because we want to select multiple items at a time so in the last step, write the selection statement multiple times for different items.

A code example is given below.

```java
public class Multiselectlist {

    public static void main(String[] args) throws
InterruptedException
    {
        WebDriverManager.chromedriver().setup();
        WebDriver driver = new ChromeDriver();
        driver.manage().window().maximize();
        driver.get("https://amolujagare.com/sample/");


        WebElement multiSel = driver.findElement(By.id("multiSel"));

        Select selMulti = new Select(multiSel);

        selMulti.selectByIndex(0);
        selMulti.selectByVisibleText("text 2");
        selMulti.selectByIndex(3);
    }
}
```

2.5 LOCATORS

To locate a web element we use findElement method e.g. driver.findElement(By.id("idname")). Here the id is a locator. There are a total of eight locators supported by selenium.

Locator	HTML Tag	Accessing using selenium
id	<input type="text" id="email" />	WebElement Element = driver.findElement(By.id("email"));
name	<input type="text" name="email" />	WebElement Element = driver.findElement(By.name("email"));
LinkText	< a href=http://google.com> My link </a>	WebElement Element = driver.findElement(By.linkText("My Link"));
Partial LinkText	< a href=http://google.com> My link </a>	WebElement Element = driver.findElement(By.partialLinkText ("My "));
TagName	<input type="text"	WebElement Element = driver.findElement(By.tagN

	name="email" />	ame ("input"));
ClassName	<input type="text" name="email" class="css"/>	WebElement Element = driver.findElement(By.className ("css"));
css elector	css=input[id=email]	WebElement Element = driver.findElement(By.cssSelector("input[id=email']"));
xpath	Click here for xpath tutorial	WebElement Element = driver.findElement(By.xpath("//tr/td "));

In the previous chapter, we have seen the use of the locator ID and the name. Let's see the other locators.

Link text: If you have a link, you can use this link text now. How do you identify that this is a link? You can locate it with the help of its HTML code with an 'a' tag in it, or you can also identify it on the webpage if you move your cursor on that particular text so you are pointer turns into a hand pointer. On this basis, you can say that this is a link. Now to find the link, we can use this link text method. The example is as below.

```
public class LinTextDemo {
  public static void main(String[] args) {
    WebDriverManager.chromedriver().setup();
    WebDriver driver = new ChromeDriver();
    driver.manage().window().maximize();
    driver.get("https://facebook.com");
    driver.findElement(By.linkText("Forgotten
password?")).click();
```

```
    }
}
```

PartialLinkText: Partial link text means a part of your link text. If your link text is very long, you can use the amount provided that the part you are using should be unique over the page. For example

```java
public class LinTextDemo {
    public static void main(String[] args) {
        WebDriverManager.chromedriver().setup();
        WebDriver driver = new ChromeDriver();
        driver.manage().window().maximize();
        driver.get("https://facebook.com");
        driver.findElement(By.partialLinkText("Forgot")).click();
    }
}
```

Class Name: Class name is also an attribute found inside a tag. You can use the class name as a locator as well. The locator class name is used quite often because the class name is generally used to give style to the element, and a common style is assigned to multiple elements so the different tags can have the same class name.

Example :
if below is the HTML tag with class name = 'CSS'

```html
<input type="text" name="email" class="css"/>
```

Then we can find the web element using the className locator as below.

```java
WebElement element
    = driver.findElement(By.className ("css"));
```

Tag Name: Tag is the first word after the angle bracket in the HTML code. It represents a particular element, for example.

```
<input type="text" name="email" class="css"/>
< a href=http://google.com> My link </a>
```

In about two examples, the tags are Input and a

We can see the element by tag name if you want to find it below.

```
WebElement element
= driver.findElement(By.tagName ("input"));
```

But generally, multiple elements on the web page acquire the same tag name, so it's best to find elements. Refer to the example explained in the find element topic.

Xpath and CSS selectors are also important locators. We will learn those in the following chapters.

2.6 XPATH

XPath is nothing but the XML path; It is a part of a particular node in a web page or inside the HTML code, just like when you have a specific file inside a folder that is there on your local drive, you have a path for that particular file below is one of the examples

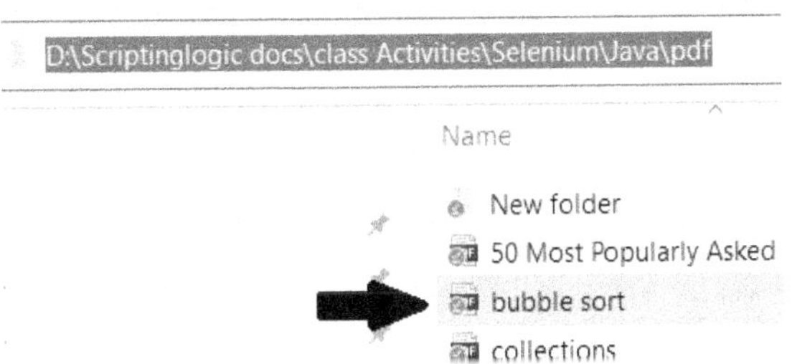

Above is the screenshot of a file located at a particular path. The path to the find bubble sort PDF is highlighted in the above screenshot.

D:\Scriptinglogic docs\class Activities\Selenium\Java\pdf

Now the path to the PDF folder starts from the D drive, which is the primary node, and with the help of the slash operator, the next node is being accessed sequentially.

The XPath is also quite like this if you consider any webpage and its HTML code.

Html is the particular form of XML

<tag>
</tag>

1. XPath of HTML
/HTML

2. XPath of body

/html/body

3. XPath head
/HTML/head

4. XPath of title
/HTML/head/title

5. XPath of center
/HTML/body/center

6. button
/HTML/body/button

7. XPath span
/HTML/body/center/span

8. XPath - p
/HTML/body/p

Absolute XPath: starting with a base parent that is HTML till that particular node
here we use the '/' single slash to access the immediate next child

Limitations of XPath
1. if the HTML page is complicated, then we will get a long string of XPath
2. if some of the web elements are removed by the developer, the earlier XPath we found will not work

Relative XPath :
1. here, we use the '//' double slash to start with
2. directly use the node (tag) that will become the XPath of that node
3. if you have multiples tags with the same tag name, then you will get multiple elements with that XPath

for example
//input

4. by default, it considers the first tag only

5. to get XPath or any other tag, we have to put some conditions in square brackets

a. //tag[1] - not recommended - it rarely works
b. //tag[@Attribute='value'] - recommended
for example : //input[@type='password']

Below is the example of An automated scenario of a login page with the help of XPath

```java
public class LoginDemoXpath {

  public static void main(String[] args) {

    WebDriverManager.chromedriver().setup();
    WebDriver driver = new ChromeDriver();

    driver.manage().window().maximize();

    driver.get("https://stock.scriptinglogic.net");

    WebElement txtUsername =
driver.findElement(By.xpath("//input[@type='text']"));
    txtUsername.sendKeys("admin");

    WebElement txtPassword =
driver.findElement(By.xpath("//input[@type='password']"));
    txtPassword.sendKeys("admin");
```

```
    WebElement btnLogin =
driver.findElement(By.xpath("//input[@value='LOG IN']"));
    btnLogin.click();
  }
}
```

Note: Instead of the tag name, you may use '*' but make sure the attribute/value pair that you are using must be unique

```
//*[@name='username']
```

If the HTML tags (node) whose XPath is to be found is in the below format

```
<tag> some text </tag>
<a href-"#"> some link </a>
<span> some text </span>
<h2> some text </h2>
<p> some text </p>
<div>some text </div>
<td>some text </td>
<font> some text </font>
<center> some text </center>
<button> submit </button>
```

We can find the web elements in the above format as below.

```
//tag[ text() = 'some text ']
```

<tag> some text </tag>
Consider the above tag with some text inside; if you have some whitespaces before or after the text, then you can use a method normalize-space() instead of text

//tag[normalize-space()='some text']

It will ignore the white spaces before or after the text.

Using contains method → substring

If you have a web element represented with
<tag> some text is there</tag>

//tag[contains (text() , 'substring of text')]

For example : //a[contains(text(),'Forgot')]

The contents method applies to the attribute also means if you have the value of attribute a long string, then you can use the contents method as below.

//tag[contains(@attribute, 'substring of the value of attribute ')]

For example :

//img[@alt = 'NLP Life Transforming Neuro Magical Stories']
we can write the above XPath as below
//img[contains(@alt , 'NLP')]

Xpath tool SelectorsHub

We have learned a lot about XPATH. Using the method we have learned earlier, you can find any XPath very easily. Still, there is one tool I can't stop myself from mentioning. Its name is SelectorsHub. An Indian invented it, 'Sanjay Kumar.' And this tool is getting more and more popular in the industry. It has several features. You can check on its official website https://selectorshub.com/. I want to mention a few features I use frequently, and I love them very much.

If you want to get that search on Google for the SelectorsHub, this is a plugin you can add to your Google Chrome. It is also available for other browsers like Firefox, Edge and Opera, etc.

Once you install it, restart your browser, and when you inspect an element somewhere, you will get the option SelectorsHub in DevTools, and from there, it will be easily able to view the xpaths.

SelectorsHub useful Feature

1. Auto-selection of XPath: Select the element on the webpage, and in the SelectorsHub tab, you will get its XPath, as shown in the screenshot.

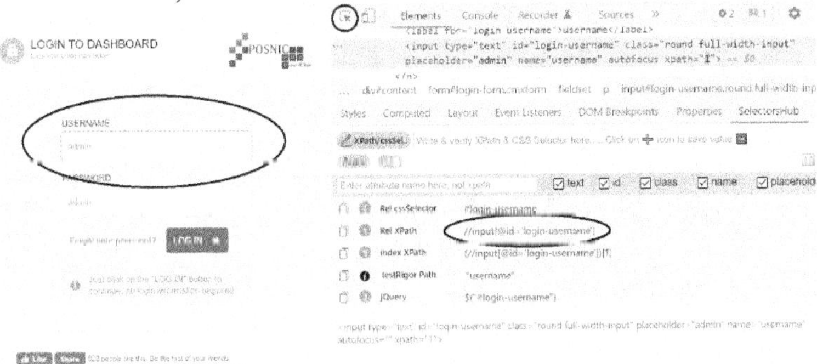

2. We get only related elements list in case of common XPath: when you inspect for any element in the inbuilt tool of any Browser, you will see the HTML code highlighted, along with the whole code

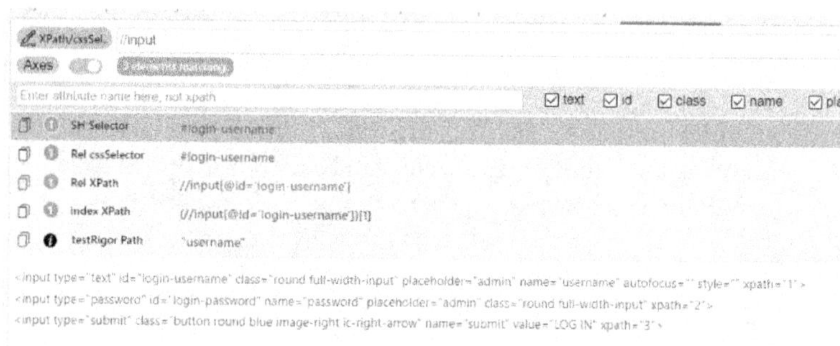

But if you use the SelectorsHub and try searching for any element, and if you have multiple such elements for the same path, then you will only see those elements, not the whole HTML code. Check the screenshot below.

1. Attribute filtration: Consider one example when I have to find the XPath of 'forgot your password link,' so I clicked on that web element and got the XPath as below. Now I don't want the XPath to include the text. Apart from it, anything else will work. So what you can do is you can untick the text, and you will get the XPath without text.

2. Similarly, you can choose whatever attribute you want by ticking/unticking the attribute. If that attribute is not available in the checkbox list given, then you can type it into the text box provided, and this will generate your XPath as per the attribute you required

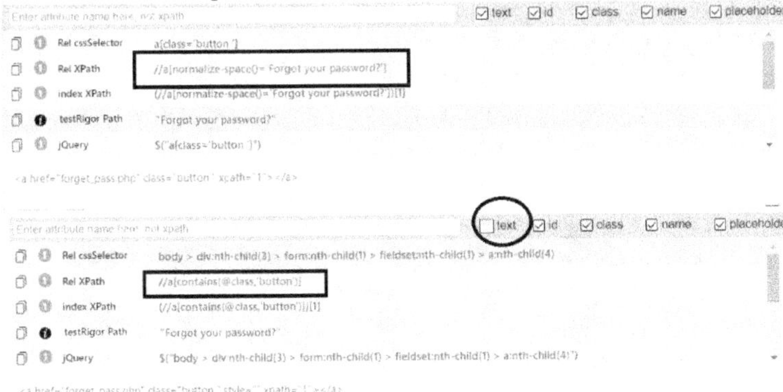

3. Set Driver command: This tool not just generates the XPATH but so many times you will come across the situation that you will have to find several elements on one particular page, so each time, you will have to write the code of find element if you set the driver command as shown in the screenshot then when you will click on the element this time it will not just give you the expert, but it will generate the whole driver command

You have to write the driver command expression, and wherever you have xpath replace that with the 'xpathvalue' keyword. For more details, you can follow the tutorial which is available right there in SelectorsHub tab in 'i' icon.

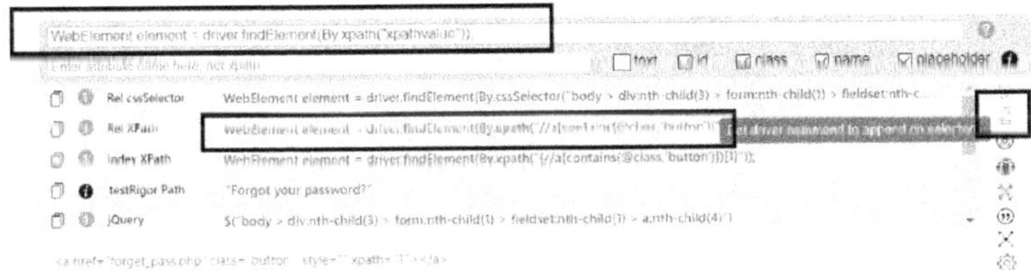

2.7 CSS SELECTORS

CSS selector is also another locator. if you have understood the expert properly, then understanding the CSS selector is not a big deal , if you want to find a CSS selector for any element on the web page, go to its tag →, e.g., → input

Check do we have an id or class
If you have an ID present for this particular tag, you can write the CSS selector in this way.

tagName#idValue

for example
input#login-username

You can skip the tag name in the case on the whole page. This ID is a unique CSS selector that will become as below
#login-username

If you have a class name present for this particular tag, then you can write the CSS selector in this way

Class → tagName.classValue
e.g. input.button

You can skip the tag name in the case on the whole page. This class value is a unique CSS selector that will become as below.

.button

3. If you want to use attributes other than id or class

tagName[attribute=value]

For E.g. → input[type=password]
Or [type=password]

Note: If your value is a single word, then there is no need to use single quotes. But if the value is a combination of a different word, that is, If in-between space is there, then you have to use the single quotes. Check below example

On the below link, there is an image with the below classpath
https://www.amazon.in/s?k=amol+ujagare.

img[alt='Practical Approach of Software Testing']

In the above example, the attribute alt has a long string as a value we can get a part of this long string using the below methods

Starts with →
 tagName[attribute^= 'Start of a string']
  → [alt^='Practical']

Ends with →
tagName[attribute$= 'end part of string']
→ [alt$='Testing']

Contains →
tagName[attribute*= 'part of string']
→ [alt*='Software']

2.8 JUNIT

Suppose we have three different test cases
1.   check the login functionality for valid input
2.   check the login functionality for invalid input
3.   check the login functionality for blank input

Suppose we are implementing these three scenarios with the help of the main function. So in the main functions, it will return these three scenarios one after the other as below.

```
public static void main()
{

    // open browser
    // maximize
    // open url
    // enter valid username
    // enter valid password
    // click login button


    --------------------------------


    // open browser
    // maximize
    // open url
    // enter invalid username
    // enter invalid password
    // click login button


    --------------------------------


    // open browser
```

```
// maximize
// open url
// enter blank username
// enter blank password
// click login button


}
```

but there are some limitations to this approach
Limitations of the main method

1. It becomes an extended code that seems like a single long test
2. There is no proper mechanism to disable any particular test
3. If in between something fails / error occurs, then it won't execute further tests
4. There is no adequate mechanism to compare actual and expected results for various data types

Now onwards, we will not use the main method. Instead, we will use an ordinary method with @Test (Annotation) at the top of the method.

 for example

```java
import org.junit.Test;

public class JunitDemo1 {

@Test
public void logintest1 ()
{
   WebDriverManager.chromedriver().setup();
   WebDriver driver = new ChromeDriver();

   driver.manage().window().maximize();

   driver.get("https://stock.scriptinglogic.net");

   WebElement txtUsername =
   driver.findElement(By.xpath("//input[@type='text']"));
```

```
    txtUsername.sendKeys("admin");

    WebElement txtPassword =
    driver.findElement(By.xpath("//input[@type='password']"));
    txtPassword.sendKeys("admin");

    WebElement btnLogin =
    driver.findElement(By.xpath("//input[@value='LOG IN']"));
    btnLogin.click();
  }
}
```

In the above class, the method logintest1() is written, wherein the login scenario is now this is not the main method. To make this method executable, we have written @Test at the top of the method. Which is an annotation, and it comes from the Junit (you have to import the Junit - You will get suggestions to import when you move your cursor to @Test)

Now, if you right-click, you will get the run option.

So in the same class, we can have multiple test methods as well as below.

```
import org.junit.Test;
public class JunitDemo1 {

  @Test
  public void logintest1()
  {
    WebDriverManager.chromedriver().setup();
    WebDriver driver = new ChromeDriver();

    driver.manage().window().maximize();

    driver.get("https://stock.scriptinglogic.net");

    WebElement txtUsername =
    driver.findElement(By.xpath("//input[@type='text']"));
    txtUsername.sendKeys("admin");
```

```java
    WebElement txtPassword =
    driver.findElement(By.xpath("//input[@type='password']"));
    txtPassword.sendKeys("admin");

    WebElement btnLogin =
    driver.findElement(By.xpath("//input[@value='LOG IN']"));
    btnLogin.click();
}

@Test
public void logintest2()
{
    WebDriverManager.chromedriver().setup();
    WebDriver driver = new ChromeDriver();

    driver.manage().window().maximize();

    driver.get("https://stock.scriptinglogic.net");

    WebElement txtUsername =
    driver.findElement(By.xpath("//input[@type='text']"));
    txtUsername.sendKeys("dsdsd");

    WebElement txtPassword =
    driver.findElement(By.xpath("//input[@type='password']"));
    txtPassword.sendKeys("dsdsds");

    WebElement btnLogin =
    driver.findElement(By.xpath("//input[@value='LOG IN']"));
    btnLogin.click();
}

@Test
public void logintest3()
{
    WebDriverManager.chromedriver().setup();
    WebDriver driver = new ChromeDriver();

    driver.manage().window().maximize();
```

```
    driver.get("https://stock.scriptinglogic.net");

    WebElement txtUsername =
    driver.findElement(By.xpath("//input[@type='text']"));
    txtUsername.sendKeys("");

    WebElement txtPassword =
    driver.findElement(By.xpath("//input[@type='password']"));
    txtPassword.sendKeys("");

    WebElement btnLogin =
    driver.findElement(By.xpath("//input[@value='LOG IN']"));
    btnLogin.click();
  }
}
```

When you run this class, all the test methods will run one after the other.

Here there are a few steps that are repetitive before the execution of the test, just like we write preconditions in test cases. Precondition has the steps which have to be executed before conducting the test.

We have annotations like

@Before - The method written below this annotation will run before every test method of the class
@After - Method return below this annotation will run after every test method of the class

See the example below.

```
import org.junit.After;
import org.junit.Before;
import org.junit.Test;
public class JunitDemo2 {
  WebDriver driver;
```

```java
@Before // method written below this annotation will run before every test
method
  public void openBrowser()
  {
    WebDriverManager.chromedriver().setup();
    driver = new ChromeDriver();
    driver.manage().window().maximize();
  }


@After // method written below, this annotation will run after every test
method
  public void closeBrowser() throws InterruptedException {
    Thread.sleep(4000);
    driver.close();
  }



@Test
public void logintest1()
{
    driver.get("https://stock.scriptinglogic.net");
        WebElement txtUsername =
        driver.findElement(By.xpath("//input[@type='text']"));
    txtUsername.sendKeys("admin");

    WebElement txtPassword =
    driver.findElement(By.xpath("//input[@type='password']"));
    txtPassword.sendKeys("admin");

    WebElement btnLogin =
    driver.findElement(By.xpath("//input[@value='LOG IN']"));
    // btnLogin.click();
}

@Test
public void logintest2()
{

    driver.get("https://stock.scriptinglogic.net");
```

```
    WebElement txtUsername =
    driver.findElement(By.xpath("//input[@type='text']"));
    txtUsername.sendKeys("dsdsd");

    WebElement txtPassword =
    driver.findElement(By.xpath("//input[@type='password']"));
    txtPassword.sendKeys("dsdsds");

    WebElement btnLogin =
    driver.findElement(By.xpath("//input[@value='LOG IN']"));
    // btnLogin.click();
  }

  @Test
  public void logintest3()
  {


    driver.get("https://stock.scriptinglogic.net");

    WebElement txtUsername =
    driver.findElement(By.xpath("//input[@type='text']"));
    txtUsername.sendKeys("");

    WebElement txtPassword =
    driver.findElement(By.xpath("//input[@type='password']"));
    txtPassword.sendKeys("");

    WebElement btnLogin =
    driver.findElement(By.xpath("//input[@value='LOG IN']"));
    // btnLogin.click();
  }
}
```

Two more annotations like

@BeforeClass - The method written below this annotation will run before the first test method of the class

@AfterClass - Method return below this annotation will run after the last test method of the class

See the example below

```java
import org.junit.*;
public class JunitDemo3 {

  static WebDriver driver;

  @BeforeClass // method written below this annotation will run before the first test method of the class
  public static void openBrowser()
  {
    WebDriverManager.chromedriver().setup();
    driver = new ChromeDriver();
    driver.manage().window().maximize();
  }

  @AfterClass // method written below this annotation will run after the last test method of the class
  public static void closeBrowser() throws InterruptedException {
    Thread.sleep(4000);
    driver.close();
  }

  @Test
  public void logintest1()
  {
    driver.get("https://stock.scriptinglogic.net");
      WebElement txtUsername =
      driver.findElement(By.xpath("//input[@type='text']"));
    txtUsername.sendKeys("admin");

    WebElement txtPassword =
    driver.findElement(By.xpath("//input[@type='password']"));
    txtPassword.sendKeys("admin");
```

```java
    WebElement btnLogin =
    driver.findElement(By.xpath("//input[@value='LOG IN']"));
    // btnLogin.click();
}

@Test
public void logintest2()
{

    driver.get("https://stock.scriptinglogic.net");

    WebElement txtUsername =
    driver.findElement(By.xpath("//input[@type='text']"));
    txtUsername.sendKeys("dsdsd");

    WebElement txtPassword =
    driver.findElement(By.xpath("//input[@type='password']"));
    txtPassword.sendKeys("dsdsds");

    WebElement btnLogin =
    driver.findElement(By.xpath("//input[@value='LOG IN']"));
    // btnLogin.click();
}

@Test
public void logintest3()
{

    driver.get("https://stock.scriptinglogic.net");

    WebElement txtUsername =
    driver.findElement(By.xpath("//input[@type='text']"));
    txtUsername.sendKeys("");

    WebElement txtPassword =
    driver.findElement(By.xpath("//input[@type='password']"));
    txtPassword.sendKeys("");
```

```
WebElement btnLogin =
driver.findElement(By.xpath("//input[@value='LOG IN']"));
//btnLogin.click();
  }
}
```

2.9 TESTNG

Junit similarity :

Like Junit, TestNG is also a framework for automating Selenium tests. To use TestNG, you must download and add the Jar of TestNG into the lib folder.

you can download the test NG jar from mvnrepository.com Open the site, search for testNG, and open the link for the latest version of TestNG. Click on the jar link on that page, and a single JAR file will be downloaded and added to your lib folder.

TestNg is considered to be more advanced than that of the unit. There are certain similarities between testNG and Junit. Those are listed below.

Description	Junit	TestNG
Test annotation	@Test	@Test
Annotation for method to be Executed before every test method	@Before	@BeforeMethod
Annotation for method to be Executed after every test method	@After	@AfterMethod

Annotation for method to be Executed before first test method of the class	@BeforeClass Method should be static	@BeforeClass Method is not static
Annotation for method to be Executed After last test method of the class	@AfterClass Method should be static	@AfterClass Method is not static

Examples codes of testNG

- with @Test (make sure here you import --> import org.testng.annotations.Test;)

```java
import io.github.bonigarcia.wdm.WebDriverManager;
import org.openqa.selenium.By;
import org.openqa.selenium.WebDriver;
import org.openqa.selenium.WebElement;
import org.openqa.selenium.chrome.ChromeDriver;
import org.testng.annotations.Test;

public class TestNGDemo1 {

@Test
public void logintest1()
{
   WebDriverManager.chromedriver().setup();
   WebDriver driver = new ChromeDriver();

   driver.manage().window().maximize();

   driver.get("https://stock.scriptinglogic.net");

   WebElement txtUsername =
driver.findElement(By.xpath("//input[@type='text']"));
   txtUsername.sendKeys("admin");
```

```java
    WebElement txtPassword =
driver.findElement(By.xpath("//input[@type='password']"));
    txtPassword.sendKeys("admin");

    WebElement btnLogin =
driver.findElement(By.xpath("//input[@value='LOG IN']"));
    btnLogin.click();
  }

  @Test
  public void logintest2()
  {
    WebDriverManager.chromedriver().setup();
    WebDriver driver = new ChromeDriver();

    driver.manage().window().maximize();

    driver.get("https://stock.scriptinglogic.net");

    WebElement txtUsername =
driver.findElement(By.xpath("//input[@type='text']"));
    txtUsername.sendKeys("dsdsd");

    WebElement txtPassword =
driver.findElement(By.xpath("//input[@type='password']"));
    txtPassword.sendKeys("dsddss");

    WebElement btnLogin =
driver.findElement(By.xpath("//input[@value='LOG IN']"));
    btnLogin.click();
  }

  @Test
  public void logintest3()
  {
    WebDriverManager.chromedriver().setup();
    WebDriver driver = new ChromeDriver();

    driver.manage().window().maximize();
```

```java
        driver.get("https://stock.scriptinglogic.net");

        WebElement txtUsername =
driver.findElement(By.xpath("//input[@type='text']"));
        txtUsername.sendKeys("");

        WebElement txtPassword =
driver.findElement(By.xpath("//input[@type='password']"));
        txtPassword.sendKeys("");

        WebElement btnLogin =
driver.findElement(By.xpath("//input[@value='LOG IN']"));
        btnLogin.click();
    }
}
```

- with @Test and @BeforeMethod & @AfterMethod

```java
import io.github.bonigarcia.wdm.WebDriverManager;
import org.openqa.selenium.By;
import org.openqa.selenium.WebDriver;
import org.openqa.selenium.WebElement;
import org.openqa.selenium.chrome.ChromeDriver;
import org.testng.annotations.AfterMethod;
import org.testng.annotations.BeforeMethod;
import org.testng.annotations.Test;

public class TestNGDemo2 {
    WebDriver driver;

    @BeforeMethod // method written below this annotation will run before every test method
    public void openBrowser()
    {
        WebDriverManager.chromedriver().setup();
        driver = new ChromeDriver();
        driver.manage().window().maximize();
    }
```

```java
@AfterMethod // method written below this annotation will run after
every test method
  public void closeBrowser() throws InterruptedException {
    Thread.sleep(4000);
    driver.close();
  }

  @Test
  public void logintest1()
  {


    driver.get("https://stock.scriptinglogic.net");

    WebElement txtUsername =
driver.findElement(By.xpath("//input[@type='text']"));
    txtUsername.sendKeys("admin");

    WebElement txtPassword =
driver.findElement(By.xpath("//input[@type='password']"));
    txtPassword.sendKeys("admin");

    WebElement btnLogin =
driver.findElement(By.xpath("//input[@value='LOG IN']"));
    btnLogin.click();
  }

  @Test
  public void logintest2()
  {


    driver.get("https://stock.scriptinglogic.net");

    WebElement txtUsername =
driver.findElement(By.xpath("//input[@type='text']"));
    txtUsername.sendKeys("dsdsd");

    WebElement txtPassword =
driver.findElement(By.xpath("//input[@type='password']"));
```

```java
    txtPassword.sendKeys("dsddss");

    WebElement btnLogin =
driver.findElement(By.xpath("//input[@value='LOG IN']"));
    btnLogin.click();
 }


 @Test
 public void logintest3()
 {

    driver.get("https://stock.scriptinglogic.net");

    WebElement txtUsername =
driver.findElement(By.xpath("//input[@type='text']"));
    txtUsername.sendKeys("");

    WebElement txtPassword =
driver.findElement(By.xpath("//input[@type='password']"));
    txtPassword.sendKeys("");

    WebElement btnLogin =
driver.findElement(By.xpath("//input[@value='LOG IN']"));
    btnLogin.click();
 }
}
```

- with @Test and @BeforeClass & @AfterClass

```java
import io.GitHub.bonigarcia.wdm.WebDriverManager;
import org.openqa.selenium.By;
import org.openqa.selenium.WebDriver;
import org.openqa.selenium.WebElement;
import org.openqa.selenium.chrome.ChromeDriver;
import org.testng.Assert;
import org.testng.annotations.*;

public class TestNGDemo3 {
  WebDriver driver;
```

```java
@BeforeClass // method written below this annotation will run before every test method
  public void openBrowser()
  {
    WebDriverManager.chromedriver().setup();
    driver = new ChromeDriver();
    driver.manage().window().maximize();
  }


@AfterClass // method written below this annotation will run after every test method
  public void closeBrowser() throws InterruptedException {
    Thread.sleep(4000);
    driver.close();
  }

  @Test
  public void logintest1()
  {

    driver.get("https://stock.scriptinglogic.net");

    WebElement txtUsername =
driver.findElement(By.xpath("//input[@type='text']"));
    txtUsername.sendKeys("admin");

    WebElement txtPassword =
driver.findElement(By.xpath("//input[@type='password']"));
    txtPassword.sendKeys("admin");

    WebElement btnLogin =
driver.findElement(By.xpath("//input[@value='LOG IN']"));
    // btnLogin.click();


  }

  @Test
  public void logintest2()
```

```java
    {

        driver.get("https://stock.scriptinglogic.net");

        WebElement txtUsername =
driver.findElement(By.xpath("//input[@type='text']"));
        txtUsername.sendKeys("dsdsd");

        WebElement txtPassword =
driver.findElement(By.xpath("//input[@type='password']"));
        txtPassword.sendKeys("dsddss");

        WebElement btnLogin =
driver.findElement(By.xpath("//input[@value='LOG IN']"));
        // btnLogin.click();
    }

    @Test
    public void logintest3()
    {

        driver.get("https://stock.scriptinglogic.net");

        WebElement txtUsername =
driver.findElement(By.xpath("//input[@type='text']"));
        txtUsername.sendKeys("");

        WebElement txtPassword =
driver.findElement(By.xpath("//input[@type='password']"));
        txtPassword.sendKeys("");

        WebElement btnLogin =
driver.findElement(By.xpath("//input[@value='LOG IN']"));
        // btnLogin.click();
    }
}

priority
enabled=false
```

2.10 TESTNG.XML

So far, we have seen that we can maintain multiple tests in one class, and when we run that class, it will run all the tests.

In testNG, we create an XML file with suite, test, and classes.

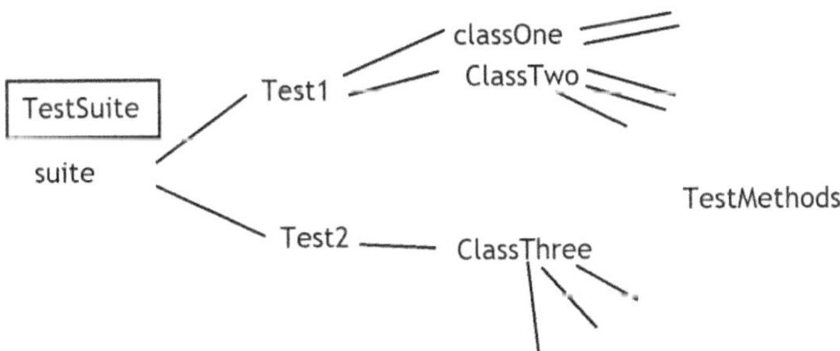

To understand this, let's create three classes in one package, each with three tests.

```java
import org.testng.annotations.Test;

public class ClassOne {

    @Test
    public void classOneTest1()
    {
        System.out.println("classOneTest1");
    }

    @Test
    public void classOneTest2()
```

```
    {
      System.out.println("classOneTest2");
    }

    @Test
    public void classOneTest3()
    {
      System.out.println("classOneTest3");
    }
}

import org.testng.annotations.Test;

public class ClassTwo {

    @Test
    public void classTwoTest1( )
    {
      System.out.println("classTwoTest1");
    }

    @Test
    public void classTwoTest2()
    {
      System.out.println("classTwoTest2");
    }

    @Test
    public void classTwoTest3()
    {
      System.out.println("classTwoTest3");
    }
}

import org.testng.annotations.Test;

public class ClassThree {

    @Test
    public void classThreeTest1( )
```

```java
    {
        System.out.println("classThreeTest1");
    }

    @Test
    public void classThreeTest2()
    {
        System.out.println("classThreeTest2");
    }

    @Test
    public void classThreeTest3()
    {
        System.out.println("classThreeTest3");
    }
}
```

After this, create a file name this as testng.xml (name testNG is not a standard name. You can write any name)

```xml
<suite name="Project name">

  <test name="module 1">
    <classes>
      <class name="Demo.ClassOne"/>
      <class name="Demo.ClassTwo"/>
    </classes>
  </test>

  <test name="module 2">
    <classes>
      <class name="Demo.ClassThree"/>
    </classes>
  </test>

</suite>
```

So suite is the parent node, specify the name to the suite, generally a project name. Inside the suite, there can be multiple test tags. Name those as your module names. Inside the test, you can write multiple classes under the tag <classes>

While including the class, make sure you mention its package path.

Now you can run this suite so sequentially that the class and the tests inside it will run.

Below is the output

classOneTest1
classOneTest2
classOneTest3
classTwoTest1
classTwoTest2
classTwoTest3
classThreeTest1
classThreeTest2
classThreeTest3

Include / exclude tags

Sometimes we have a lot of classes, and each class has a lot of tests in it, and let's say we don't want to execute a few tests in it, so we have an option of 'include tag.' I am making some changes in the above testng.xml, and let's check its output

```
<suite name="Project name">

  <test name="module 1">
    <classes>
      <class name="TestNGDemo.Demo2.ClassOne">
        <methods>
          <exclude name="classOneTest1"/>
          <exclude name="classOneTest2"/>
        </methods>
      </class>
      <class name="TestNGDemo.Demo2.ClassTwo"/>
    </classes>
```

```xml
    </test>

  <test name="module 2">
    <classes>
       <class name="TestNGDemo.Demo2.ClassThree"/>
    </classes>
  </test>

</suite>
```

Below is the output
classOneTest3
classTwoTest1
classTwoTest2
classTwoTest3
classThreeTest1
classThreeTest2
classThreeTest3

```xml
  <class name="TestNGDemo.Demo2.ClassOne">
        <methods>
          <exclude name="classOneTest1"/>
          <exclude name="classOneTest2"/>
        </methods>
      </class>
```

this shows that you can exclude some specific methods from a class using exclude tag, on the contrary if use include tag this will only include the included test and will ignore the other tests check the code and output below

```xml
<suite name="Project name">

  <test name="module 1">
    <classes>
       <class name="TestNGDemo.Demo2.ClassOne">
          <methods>
            <include name="classOneTest1"/>
          </methods>
```

```
      </class>
      <class name="TestNGDemo.Demo2.ClassTwo"/>
    </classes>
  </test>

  <test name="module 2">
    <classes>
      <class name="TestNGDemo.Demo2.ClassThree"/>
    </classes>
  </test>

</suite>
```

output :
classOneTest1
classTwoTest1
classTwoTest2
classTwoTest3
classThreeTest1
classThreeTest2
classThreeTest3

include exclude groups

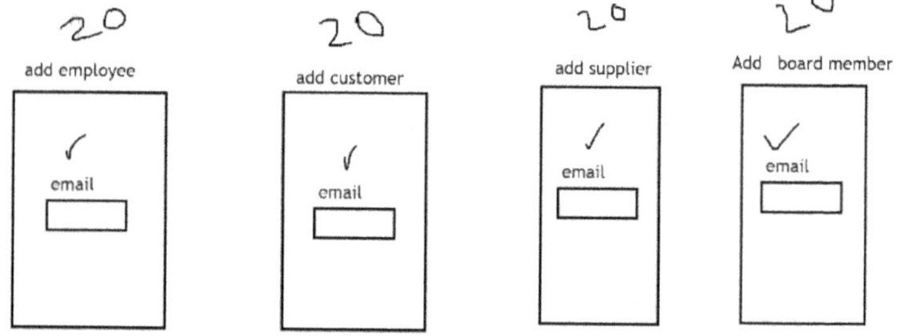

Consider a scenario where you have four classes. Each class has an average of 20 test cases, and every class has one of the test cases based on email validation. Suppose the developer is your friend, and the developer comes to you and says whatever test cases you have written, do execute them, but do not execute the test cases where you are validating the email format. Because of this part, I have not implemented this yet. If you run your test cases now, there will be failures. And unnecessarily, there would be bugs raised, so better wait for some time. Once I complete it, you can test it.

In this case, we will require much effort to apply the include and exclude. What we will do is we will group such a test, and we can include or exclude the group. How to let's see this

- All the test cases which fall under the carrot category of email validation put them into one group as below

```
@Test (groups = "email")
public void classThreeTest2()
{
   System.out.println("classThreeTest2");
}
```

- Add below code snippet into your testng.xml

```
<groups>
  <run>
    <exclude name="email"/>
  </run>
</groups>
```

The complete code will look like below

```
<suite name="Project name">

<groups>
  <run>
    <exclude name="email"/>
  </run>
</groups>

  <test name="module 1">
    <classes>
      <class name="TestNGDemo.Demo2.ClassOne">
        <methods>
          <include name="classOneTest1"/>
```

```
        </methods>
      </class>
      <class name="TestNGDemo.Demo2.ClassTwo"/>
    </classes>
  </test>

  <test name="module 2">
    <classes>
      <class name="TestNGDemo.Demo2.ClassThree"/>
    </classes>
  </test>

</suite>

output :
classOneTest1
classTwoTest1
classTwoTest3
classThreeTest1
classThreeTest3
```

So in the above output, you can observe that the second test is skipped because the group is equal to the email for every second test we have added.

2.11 ASSERTS

Until now, we have learned lots of concepts from Selenium, but everywhere, whatever we have implemented is just automation, not automation testing. I am saying this because you are testing will be said to be completed when you compare actual and expected results, and till now, we have never done that, so in this chapter, we are going to study how to compare actual and expected results and get the status of your test not for this we have to assert
Assert is available in testNG and Junit but with a little difference. Now I will demonstrate your Asserts concerning testNG, and at the end, I will explain the difference between testNG assert and Junit assert.

Suppose there is a login page, and I am entering the correct username and password, and I can reach the dashboard, So my test is passed or failed? Yes, it is passed.

In the second scenario, I am entering an incorrect username and password and getting the error message that my test is passed or failed. Yes, it is still passed because when you enter in the correct username and incorrect password, your expected result should be an error message.

Let's come back to the first scenario.
We have entered the correct username and password and can reach the dashboard. When we test this manually, there is some observation based on which we compare the expected result with the actual and pass the judgment that the test is passed.

Now what could be our observation in this scenario

1. A page title is changed
2. URL is changed
3. We can see the text dashboard on the web page

Let's see how to set this as an expected result, get the actual result, and finally compare them. Below is the login code

```java
@Test
public void logintest1()
{
  WebDriverManager.chromedriver().setup();
  WebDriver driver = new ChromeDriver();

  driver.manage().window().maximize();

  driver.get("https://stock.scriptinglogic.net");

  WebElement txtUsername =
driver.findElement(By.xpath("//input[@type='text']"));
  txtUsername.sendKeys("admin");

  WebElement txtPassword =
driver.findElement(By.xpath("//input[@type='password']"));
  txtPassword.sendKeys("admin");

  WebElement btnLogin =
driver.findElement(By.xpath("//input[@value='LOG IN']"));
  btnLogin.click();
}
}
```

1. Let's see how to use the page title as the expected result and compare it with the actual result.

```java
String expected = "POSNIC - Dashboard";
String actual = driver.getTitle();

Assert.assertEquals(actual,expected,"this is not a dashboard");
```

(The third parameter message is optional)
The above code explains my expected result, and to check the page title, we have already learned the getTitle() method. We have an assertEqual() method, which can compare two similar types of elements; here, it is comparing two strings.

1. Let's see how to use URL as the expected result and compare it with the actual result.

String expected =
"https://stock.scriptinglogic.net/dashboard.php";
String actual = driver.getCurrentUrl();

Assert.*assertEquals*(actual,expected,"this is not a dashboard");
(The third parameter message is optional)
The above code explains my expected result, and to check the Url, we have already learned the getCurrentUrl() method.

1. Let's see how to use Dashboard text as the expected result and compare it with the actual result.

String expected = "Dashboard";

Here the expected result is the dashboard in the form of a string. Now to get the actual result, we need to find the element holding the text dashboard and grab the text out of it.

WebElement dashboard =
driver.findElement(By.*cssSelector*(".active-tab"))

You can see that we have captured the dashboard element using any locator using the above code. Now to catch the text out of it, we have a method getText()

so dashboard.getText() will give me the text at this place

In this case, where you expect some text to be available on the web page (here it is the dashboard), sometimes there would be a challenge. The element you are trying to find which contains your expected text may be unavailable on the page, or you have not reached the desired page, and here the desired element is not there. In that case, the finite element method will throw an exception. And no, for it will execute the statement subsequently, the assert statement will not execute, and you will not get an abortion to see the comparison between the actual and expected result. For that, we will handle the exception using try catch.

Refer below code

```
@Test public void logintest1() {
  WebDriverManager.chromedriver().setup();
  WebDriver driver = new ChromeDriver();

  driver.manage().window().maximize();

  driver.get("https://stock.scriptinglogic.net");

  WebElement txtUsername =
driver.findElement(By.xpath("//input[@type='text']"));
  txtUsername.sendKeys("admin1");

  WebElement txtPassword =
driver.findElement(By.xpath("//input[@type='password']"));
  txtPassword.sendKeys("admin");

  WebElement btnLogin =
driver.findElement(By.xpath("//input[@value='LOG IN']"));
  btnLogin.click();

//------------- Assertion code ----------
  String expected = "Dashboard";
  String actual = "";
  try {
     actual = driver.findElement(By.cssSelector(".active-
tab")).getText();
  } catch (Exception e) {

  }
Assert.assertEquals(actual,expected,"This is not a dashboard");
```

}
Now we will consider a scenario where I enter an incorrect username and password and get the error message "wrong username or password."
My expected result would be the text "wrong username or password." Also, we are about to verify a text on a web page, so just like the procedure we followed for the dashboard, we will first find the web element that holds this text. We will grab the text out of it. Then we will compare it with the actual result for the safe side finding element we will keep inside the try-catch block. Refer to the code below.

```
String expected = "Wrong Username or Password";
String actual = "";

try {
    actual = driver.findElement(By.cssSelector(".error-box")).getText();
}
catch (Exception e)
{

}

System.out.println("Expected-"+expected);
System.out.println("Actual="+actual);

Assert.assertEquals(actual,expected,"incorrect error message or error message absent");
```

2.12 REPORTS

In recent chapters, we have seen how to generate testng.xml. Here we are going to see a few of the reports that we will generate if we add a small code snippet into our testng.xml

Emailable reports: Add the below code snippet into your testng.xml and run the XML file. After execution, you will get the information generated as below

Code Snippet to add in the testnng.xml

```xml
<listeners>
  <listener class-
name="org.testng.reporters.EmailableReporter2" />
</listeners>
```

TestNg.xml file will look like this

```xml
<suite name="All sites">

  <listeners>
    <listener class-
name="org.testng.reporters.EmailableReporter2" />
  </listeners>

  <test name="study sites">
    <classes>
      <class name ="TestNGDemos.Sites.JobSites"/>
      <class name
="TestNGDemos.Sites.TutorialsSites"/>
    </classes>
  </test>
```

```
<test name = "Social sites">
  <classes>
    <class name="TestNGDemos.Sites.SocialSites"/>
  </classes>

</test>

</suite>
```

Reports will look like this

Test	# Passed	# Skipped	# Retried	# Failed	Time (ms)	Included Groups	Excluded Groups
All sites							
study sites	7	0	0	1	57,171		
Social sites	2	0	0	0	9,275		
Total	9	0	0	1	66,446		

Class	Method	Start	Time (ms)
All sites			
study sites — failed			
TestNGDemos.Sites.TutorialsSites	tutorialpoints	1649647780385	2975
study sites — passed			
TestNGDemos.Sites.JobSites	monster	1649647734386	14145
	naukri	1649647731193	3189
	shine	1649647763572	3843
	timesjobs	1649647748531	15039
TestNGDemos.Sites.TutorialsSites	javatpoint	1649647770057	4584
	scriptinglogic	1649647774641	5744
	w3scools	1649647783367	1101
Social sites — passed			
TestNGDemos.Sites.SocialSites	Instagram	1649647787076	1480
	facebook	1649647788557	1072

In this report, at the top, you see 'all sites.' it is the suite name. Below this, you see study sites and social sites. These are the two test tags. In that, you can see the number of passed test cases and the number of field test cases. Below that, you will see the total of it.

The table below shows that each test tag has some classes. First, it will show failed classes. Then it will show Pass classes. If you click on the failed class, it will redirect you to the error message below

TestNGDemos.Sites.TutorialsSites#tutorialpoints

```
java.lang.AssertionError: this is not tutorials website expected [https://www.tutorialspoint.com/index.htm] but found
        at TestNGDemos.Sites.TutorialsSites.tutorialpoints(TutorialsSites.java:42)
        at java.base/java.util.ArrayList.forEach(ArrayList.java:1541)
        at com.intellij.rt.testng.IDEARemoteTestNG.run(IDEARemoteTestNG.java:66)
        at com.intellij.rt.testng.RemoteTestNGStarter.main(RemoteTestNGStarter.java:109)
... Removed 29 stack frames
```

ReportNG reports :

Now, these are the third-party report to generate these reports. You must have below three jar files

guice-3.0.jar
reporting-1.1.4.jar
velocity-dep-1.4.jar

Add these jar files to your library, and you can add the below code snippet to your suit and the report. It will generate the reports.

Add the below code to your suit tag. As you can see, we have added it to the emailable reports.

```
<listeners>
    <listener class-
name="org.uncommons.reportng.HTMLReporter"/>
    <listener class-
name="org.uncommons.reportng.JUnitXMLReporter"/>
 </listeners>
```

Below are the reports screenshots

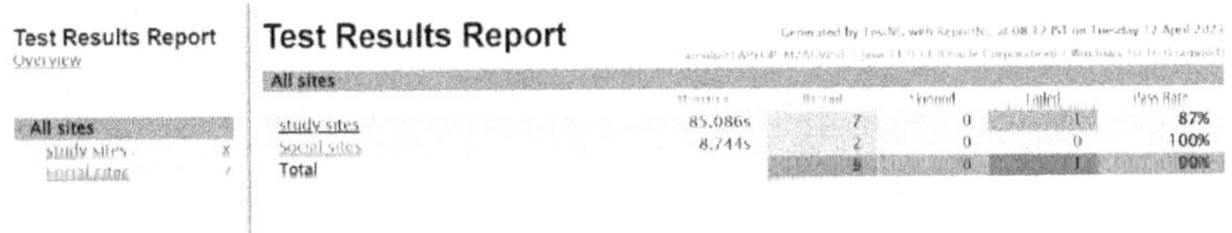

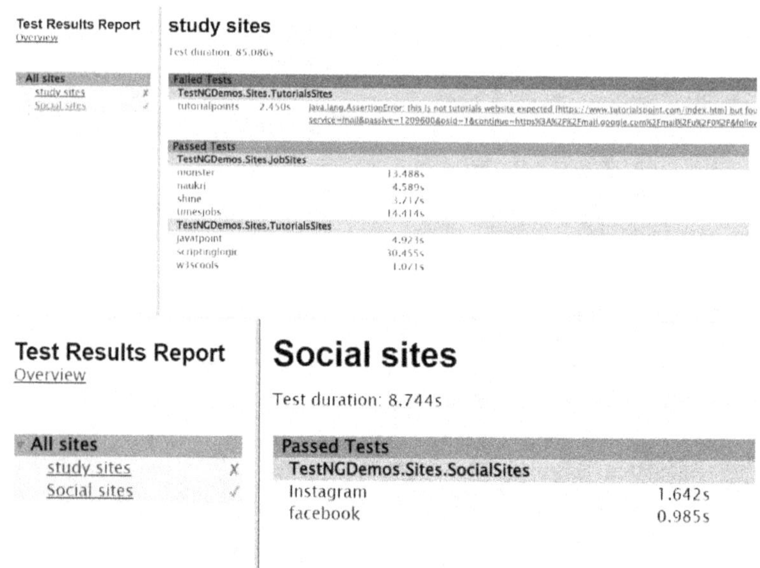

Taking screenshots

Screenshots are essential to maintain as proof of your bugs. In automation using Selenium, we have a few simple steps with the help of which we can take the screenshot very quickly. Below are the actions and code given

1. create the object reference of TakesScreenshot interface assign the current driver to it, typecast it to TakesScreenshot

```
TakesScreenshot ts = (TakesScreenshot) driver;
```

2. using the object reference ts call the method getScreenshotAs()

```
File scrFile = ts.getScreenshotAs(OutputType.FILE);
```

We have to create a unique file name for each screenshot. It means the screenshot created must have a different filename for each screenshot image file, and this we can achieve by attaching the timestamp to the filename.

```
String timeStamp = new
SimpleDateFormat("_yyyyMMdd_hhmmss").format(new Date());
String fileName= "IMG"+timeStamp+".png";
```

3. copy this file object into a real file

```java
FileUtils.copyFile(scrFile,new File("D:\\screenshots\\"+fileName));
```

The complete code is as below

```java
public class ScreenshotDemo {

    @Test
    public void  loginTest1() throws IOException {
        WebDriverManager.chromedriver().setup();
        WebDriver driver = new ChromeDriver();
        driver.manage().window().maximize();
        driver.get("https://linkedin.com/");

        TakesScreenshot ts = (TakesScreenshot) driver;

        File scrFile = ts.getScreenshotAs(OutputType.FILE);

        String timeStamp = new
SimpleDateFormat("_yyyyMMdd_hhmmss").format(new Date());
        String fileName= "IMG"+timeStamp+".png";

        FileUtils.copyFile(scrFile,new
File("D:\\screenshots\\"+fileName));

    }
}
```

Below is the generated screenshot with its file name

IMG_20220412_083034

Extent reports

To generate an 'extent report,' first of all, we need to add the latest jar of the extent report. Search on google for 'extent report 5 jar download.'

You will get the link to download the jars.

for e.g.
https://jar-download.com/artifacts/com.aventstack/extentreports/5.0.9

Get all the jars and put them into the libraries of your project.

Now let's see how to write a code to generate an extent report.

First, we must create an extent report object and load it with certain information.

So let's create the object of ExtentReports along with that, we will need one more object: ExtendSparkReporter this object will need to set the report file path.

ExtentSparkReporter reporter = new ExtentSparkReporter("Report/report.html");

Here we have mentioned the path to the report file.

ExtentReports extent = new ExtentReports();

Now we have to attach this reporter object to the ExtentReport object as below.

extent.attachReporter(reporter);

Now below steps are optional but essential. This will help us to set some information on the report.

reporter.config().setDocumentTitle("Stock Management system");
reporter.config().setReportName("Regression testing report");

Two statements will set the document title and report the name, respectively.

The below steps will set some information about your project inside your report. You can have as many setSystemInfo as you can, and you can write any key-value pair into it that describes your project information.

```
extent.setSystemInfo("Project name","Stock Management");
extent.setSystemInfo("Developers name","Amar");
extent.setSystemInfo("Testers name","Ashish");
extent.setSystemInfo("Company","Infosys");
extent.setSystemInfo("Project Deadline","12-12-2022");
```

We prefer to maintain this whole code inside the @Beforeclass method as below.

```
ExtentReports extent;

@BeforeClass
public void initExtentReport()
{
   ExtentSparkReporter reporter = new
ExtentSparkReporter("Report/report.html");
   ExtentReports extent = new ExtentReports();
   extent.attachReporter(reporter);

   reporter.config().setDocumentTitle("Stock Management
system");
   reporter.config().setReportName("Regression testing report");

   extent.setSystemInfo("Project name","Stock Management");
   extent.setSystemInfo("Developers name","Amar");
   extent.setSystemInfo("Testers name","Ashish");
   extent.setSystemInfo("Company","Infosys");
   extent.setSystemInfo("Project Deadline","12-12-2022");
}
```

Now we are all set to generate the extent report next phase. Inside each test, you have to create the object of the ExtentTest this will specify the test name. Also, using this test object, we can generate different logs. Check the highlighted code below.

```java
@Test
public void loginTest1() throws IOException {
    ExtentTest test = extent.createTest("valid login Test");

    WebDriverManager.chromedriver().setup();
    WebDriver driver = new ChromeDriver();
    driver.manage().window().maximize();
    driver.get("https://stock.scriptinglogic.net/");

    test.info("url is opened");

    System.out.println(driver.findElement(By.cssSelector("[for=login-username]")).getText());

    WebElement txtUser =
    driver.findElement(By.cssSelector("#login-username"));
    txtUser.sendKeys("admin");

    test.info("username is set");

    WebElement txtPass =
    driver.findElement(By.cssSelector("#login-password"));
    txtPass.sendKeys("admin");

    test.info("password is set");

    WebElement btnLogin = driver.findElement(By.cssSelector(".ic-right-arrow"));
    btnLogin.click();

    test.info("login button is clicked");
}
```

We must call the function using the object extent to write the report, which we will maintain in the after-class method below.

```java
@AfterClass
public void writeToReport()
{
  extent.flush();
}
```

This will generate the single test report as below

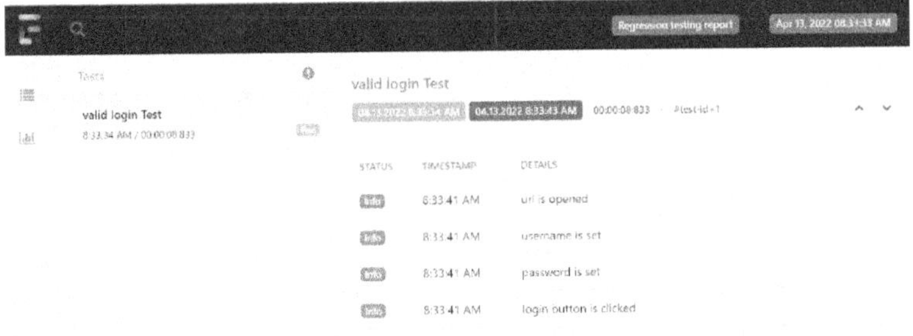

The system information is generated as below

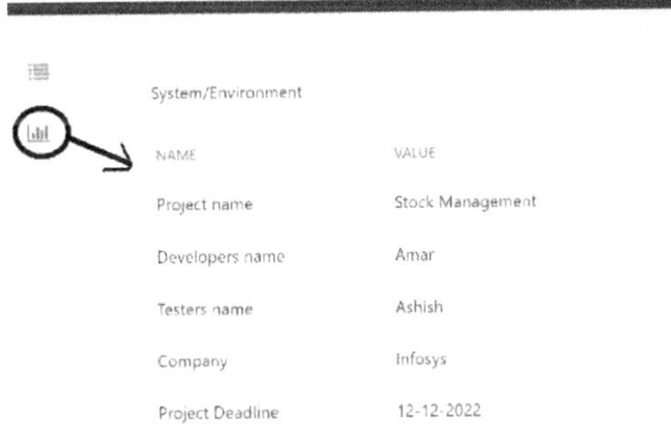

Here, we have not set the pass-fail criteria, 'asserts' can set it. Let's add the asserts here and see how the code becomes

Add the below code after the script to click on the login button.

```java
String expected
="https://stock.scriptinglogic.net/dashboard.php";
String actual = driver.getCurrentUrl();
```

```
try {
  Assert.assertEquals(actual, expected, "This is not a dashboard");
  test.pass("I am on dashboard (test is passed)");
}
catch (AssertionError e)
{
  test.fail(e.getMessage());
}
```

Here we have written a log test. pass() after the successful execution of the assert equals method.

If the test fails assertEquals() method throws an exception. It throws the assertionError exception. So we are catching that inside the catch block. And using the exception object, we are getting the message and printing it on the report. using the method e.getMessage() placed inside test.fail()

In the report, we will get the below things.

STATUS	TIMESTAMP	DETAILS
Info	8:33:55 AM	url is opened
Info	8:33:55 AM	username is set
Info	8:33:55 AM	password is set
Info	8:33:55 AM	login button is clicked
Fail	8:33:56 AM	This is not a login page expected [https://stock.scriptinglogic.net1] but found [https://stock.scriptinglogic.net/index.php?msg=Wrong%20Username%20or%20Password&type=error]

Attaching screenshots to the extent report

To attach screenshots in an 'extent report' there is an inbuilt method addScreenCapturFromPath().This method does not take the screenshot but attaches an image to your report from a particular path.

Now your job is to create a screenshot and generate a path that you can add to the addScreenCapturFromPath() method, which will add the screenshot to the corresponding report.

For this, we will create a method that will generate a screenshot and return the filename. Below is the method

```java
public static String takingScreenshot(WebDriver driver) throws IOException {

    TakesScreenshot ts = (TakesScreenshot) driver;
    File scrFile = ts.getScreenshotAs(OutputType.FILE);

    String timeStamp = new SimpleDateFormat("_yyyyMMdd_hhmmss").format(new Date());
    String fileName= "IMG"+timeStamp+".png";

    FileUtils.copyFile(scrFile,new File("Report\\screenshots\\"+fileName));

    return fileName;
}
```

The screenshot code is written in the above method, which we have already seen in this chapter. The only difference here is that the code is written inside the method, and the method's return type is a string. Because We want to get the image's filename, the method is public so that I can access it outside the packages. The method is static as well, because of which I will not need any object to call this method.

We need a driver object to create the TakesScreenshots object reference, so this driver object I am taking as an argument through this method.

Now, this method takes the screenshot and holds the file name. We can add the below statement in the extent report code whenever you need a screenshot.

```java
test.addScreenCaptureFromPath("./screenshots/"+takingScreenshot(
```

driver));

Note: here, while creating the screenshots method, we have created a folder in reports names as screenshots. Refer to the screenshot method above. The screenshots are getting stored inside the screenshot folder. Hence this method will generate the above path for a particular screenshot.

2.13 DATA DRIVEN FRAMEWORK

Suppose we have to write a script for a login test on the login page. There are two fields, username, and password, so with the below steps
1. open the browser
2. open the URL
3. enter the username
4. enter the password
5. Click on the login button

these are the steps we have, so here we can have different scenarios with the same steps as below
1. to test the functionality of the login button for valid Input
2. to test the functionality of the login button for invalid Input
3. To test the functionality of the login button for blank Input
4. to test the functionality of the login button for another username and password

The test steps are the same, but the test input is different. One approach is to create various tests with different data, but the code will be redundant in this case. Instead, we propose to use a data provider where we will write the test only once, and there will be a method that will provide data to your test.

That's called a data provider, and this is nothing but a data-driven framework.

Data Provider using array

As we have said, we will provide data for the login test.

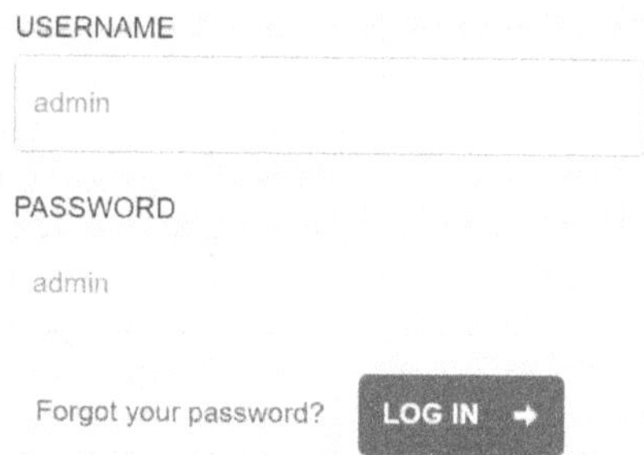

And we want to use the below data for the login test. The single login test should run four times for four different inputs.

	0	1
0	admin	admin
1	invlaid-1	invlaid-1
2	invlaid-2	invlaid-2
3	invlaid-3	invlaid-3

This Input will maintain in one method return type will be a two-dimensional object array as below
Note: above the method, @DataProvider annotation is there


```java
@DataProvider
public Object[][] getData()
{
   Object[][] data = new Object[4][2]; // row x col


   data[0][0] = "admin";
   data[0][1] = "admin"; // 1st row
```

```
data[1][0] = "invalid-1";
data[1][1] = "invalid-1";  // 2nd row


data[2][0] = "invalid-2";
data[2][1] = "invalid-2";  // 3rd row


data[3][0] = "invalid-3";
data[3][1] = "invalid-3";  // 4th row



  return  data;
}
```

Now let's see how to use this for the loginTest

```
@Test (dataProvider = "getData")
public void loginTest(String username,String password)
{
  WebDriverManager.chromedriver().setup();
  WebDriver driver = new ChromeDriver();


  driver.manage().window().maximize();
  driver.get("https://stock.scriptinglogic.net/");


  WebElement txtUser =
driver.findElement(By.xpath("//input[@id='login-username']"));
  txtUser.sendKeys(username);


  WebElement txtPassword =
driver.findElement(By.xpath("//input[@id='login-password']"));
  txtPassword.sendKeys(password);
```

```
    WebElement btnLogin =
driver.findElement(By.xpath("//input[@type='submit']"));
    btnLogin.click();


}
```

In the above program, you will observe three changes to a standard test

- in front of the @Test tag, we have written (dataProvider = "getData")
  now get data is the name of the method
- we have passed two parameters into the method loginTest(String username, String password)
- the parameter variables are used at the place where the username and password are required in sendkeys
  txtUser.sendKeys(username);
  txtPassword.sendKeys(password);

Data Provider using Excel sheet

In the above example, we have seen how to send the data using a data provider that stores the data in the array. Now we will keep this data in an excel sheet, and this Excel sheet we will use as the data provider.

Here I understand one thing: ultimately, we will follow the same procedure. We will only provide data through the getData() method through the array. We will read the Excel sheet and each cell value and assign that cell value to the corresponding place in the array.

To read from the Excel sheet, we need to download the POI library and add all the jars to our lib folder. you can download this from below official link https://poi.apache.org/

Create one Excel sheet and store it at some location in windows. It is better to keep inside your project only suppose that I have created the Excel sheet which has below data.

	0	1
0	admin	admin
1	invlaid-1	invlaid-1
2	invlaid-2	invlaid-2
3	invlaid-3	invlaid-3

to read the Excel sheet, below are the steps

- Read the file using FileInputStream
FileInputStream fis = new
FileInputStream("Data/MyData2.xlsx");
"Data/MyData2.xlsx" this is → path to excel file

- Create the object below
XSSFWorkbook workbook = new XSSFWorkbook(fis);

The class XSSFWorkbook is coming from the POI library.
The file object is converted to the workbook object.

- Excel sheets can have multiple sheets in them now. Which sheet we are working with that we have to identify first. The below statement creates a sheet object and gets us the sheet.

```
XSSFSheet sheet = workbook.getSheet("Sheet1");
```

- Now let's count the active number of rows of this sheet
  `int rowCount = sheet.getPhysicalNumberOfRows();`

- Now that we got the number of rows, we can now create the two-dimensional object array as below

```
Object[][] data = new Object[rowCount][2];
```

Here rows count can be variable, but the columns will be fixing that too because this is a login page, so only two inputs are getting sent, so column count two is fixed

- Now let's traverse through all the rows and get each cell value from each row using for loop

```
for (int i = 0; i < rowCount; i++)
{
  XSSFRow row = sheet.getRow(i);

  data[i][0] = row.getCell(0).toString().trim();
  data[i][1] = row.getCell(1).toString().trim();
}
```

- The for loop traverse from 0 to rowCount. Inside it, we are capturing the row object using sheet.getRow(i) method.
- Whatever value of the 'i' would be there during that iteration, it will pick up the corresponding row, and we can get each cell value using row.getCell() method.
- And we will store that in the array as shown in the above code.

toString() method: It is used to convert the object returned by the getCell() method into the string

trim() method: It is optionally used to remove any white spaces before or after the cell value
e.g., = "admin," this will be trimmed as "admin."

The complete code is as below
@DataProvider
public Object[][] getData() throws IOException {

```
        FileInputStream fis = new
FileInputStream("Data/MyData2.xlsx");
        XSSFWorkbook workbook = new XSSFWorkbook(fis);
        XSSFSheet sheet = workbook.getSheet("Sheet1");
        int rowCount = sheet.getPhysicalNumberOfRows();

Object[][] data = new Object[rowCount][2];


        for (int i = 0; i < rowCount; i++) {
        XSSFRow row = sheet.getRow(i);
data[i][0] = row.getCell(0).toString().trim();
data[i][1] = row.getCell(1).toString().trim();


        }
    return data;
}
```

What if we have headers in the excel

Sometimes we may have headers in Excel where you have stored the data as below.

Username	Password
admin	admin
invlaid-1	invlaid-1
invlaid-2	invlaid-2
invlaid-3	invlaid-3

In this case, the first row does not contain actual values. The values start from the second row, that is, the first index row.

Same has to be picked up and to the object array that we will create inside the data provider.

It means the First row of the Excel sheet will be the 0th row of an array, and so on. To implement this, we will have to make three changes as below

- Object[][] data = new Object[rowCount-1][2];

Because rowCount will give us the total number of rows in the Excel sheet, whereas in array in we don't need the header row, so we are subtracting one from the row count

- for (int i = 0; i<rowCount-1;i++)
  As the total number of rows in the array is rowCount -1 so the fall look will also help drivers till rowCount -1

- HSSFRow row = sheet.getRow(i+1);
  This statement is inside the for a loop. In for loop, 'i' starts from zero. If we take 'i' as it is in getRow() method, that is getRow(i), then getRow() method will attempt to access the 0th row of an excel sheet. But the 0th row of an excel sheet is the header, and we don't want that. So we are adding 1 in with 'i' that is › sheet.getRow(i+1);

The complete code is as below

```java
@DataProvider
public Object[][] getData() throws IOException {

        FileInputStream fis = new FileInputStream("Data/MyData2.xlsx");
        XSSFWorkbook workbook = new XSSFWorkbook(fis);
        XSSFSheet sheet = workbook.getSheet("Sheet1");
        int rowCount = sheet.getPhysicalNumberOfRows();

Object[][] data = new Object[rowCount-1][2];
        for (int i = 0; i < rowCount-1; i++) {
        XSSFRow row = sheet.getRow(i+1);
            data[i][0] = row.getCell(0).toString().trim();
            data[i][1] = row.getCell(1).toString().trim();



    }
    return data;
}
```

2.14 PAGE OBJECT MODEL

What is a framework :

We say that the Page object model is a framework, so what is a Framework? Framework, in simple words, is used to organize things. The word Framework is not used explicitly for the software industry. It is used in every other sector. For example, we have business frameworks.

Frameworks organize things. The best example is your house. You might be living in an apartment or a row house, in your house you have different rooms like kitchen, bedroom, hall. You will never have just one large area in one house. We will always have rooms. Because the things to be kept in the kitchen are held in the kitchen. The things to be kept in the bedroom are kept in the bedroom. The things to be kept in the hall are kept in the hall. In this way, any framework will organize things very properly.

Similarly, it is always good to use a framework if we want to maintain our many tests. Now we will study this page object model, which is getting increasingly popular.

So let's understand this using the below diagram.

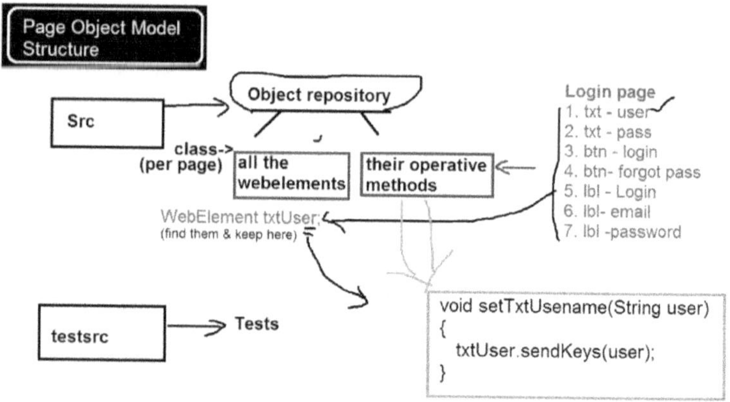

The above diagram explains the central idea of the page object model. It has two sections source and test source. In the search section, we maintain the object repository. What is the object repository? It has all the web elements and their actions. Here we will not preserve any tests, just the web element and their actions. We will maintain one class for each page of your project so let's create a project and see how this can be implemented.

This project we will implement in Maven.

If we are creating a project using Maven, we have two advantages

1.   We get a ready framework (ready folder structure)
2.   We will not need to maintain the lib folder for storing all the jars/libraries

We will see the Maven project creation in both the editors, that is, IntelliJ idea and Eclipse, and we will see the steps in IntelliJ Idea.

Maven project creation in IntelliJ Idea

1. Open intellij idea
2. Click on file → new → project

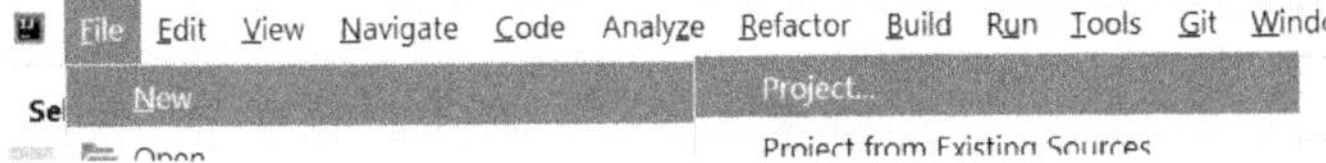

3. Select maven select create from archetype

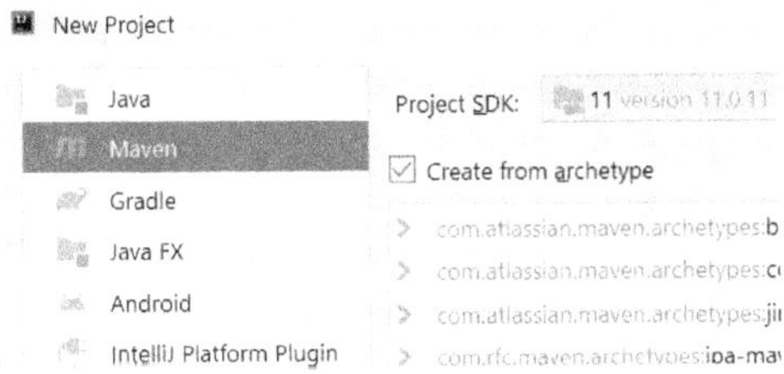

4. Select maven-archetyepe-quicksart and click next

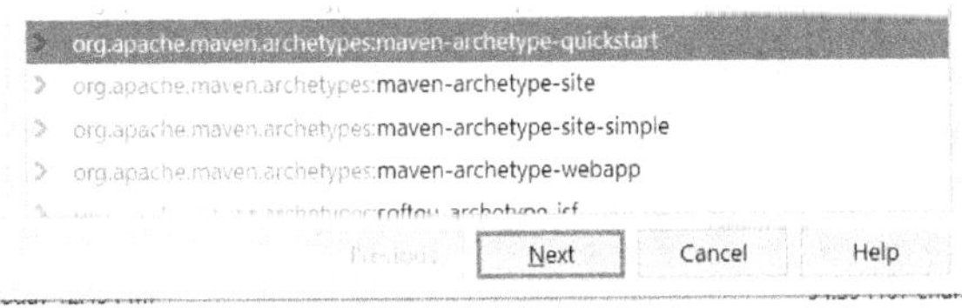

5. name the project

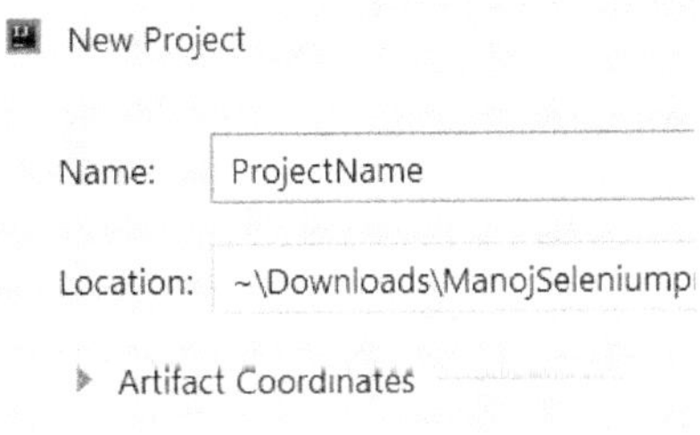

6. click next and finish

wait for a few minutes, and it will create your project
here you will get two sections under src → main and test

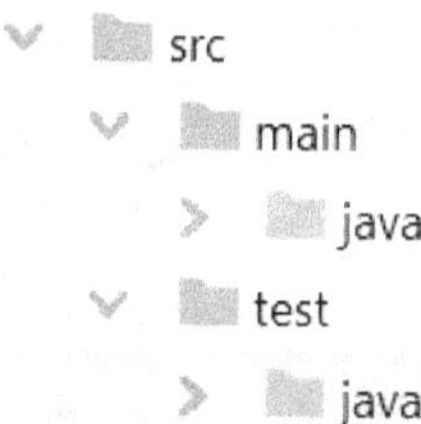

We will maintain the object repository in the main section, and in the test section, we will maintain all the tests.

The next important thing is the pom.xml file.

Here we have to add dependencies of → selenium, TestNG,webdrivermanager, and all the libraries we added in the previous project as jar files.

For that, go to https://mvnrepository.com/

And search for the dependencies below.

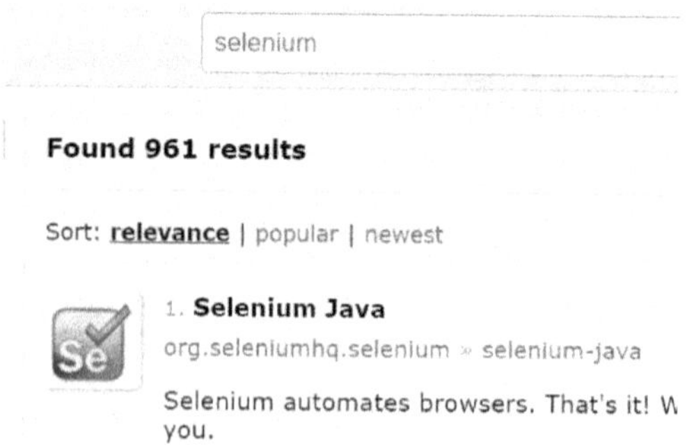

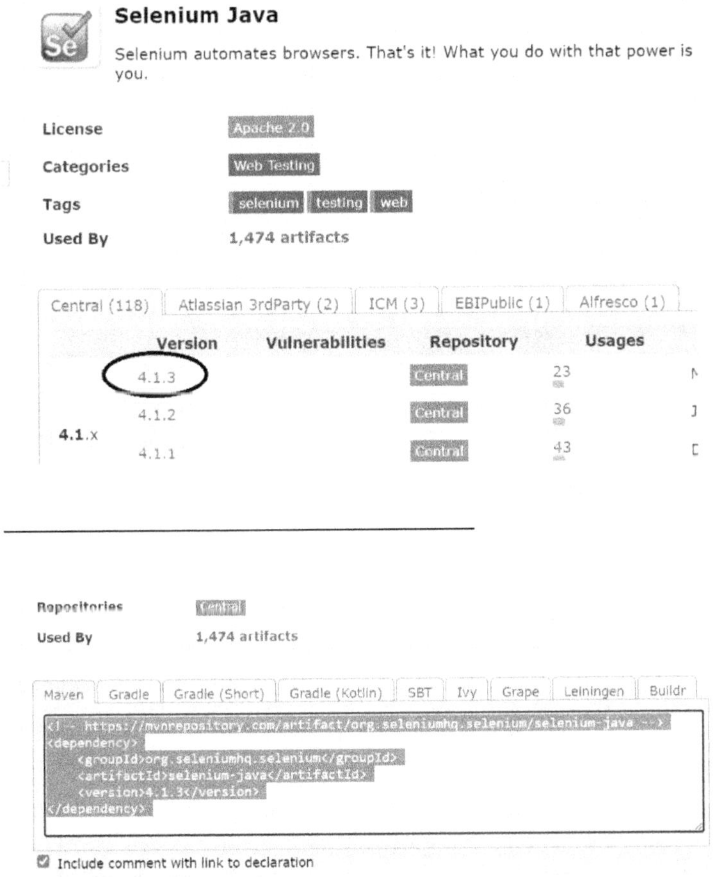

Similarly, get the other dependencies, and you have to add these code snippets inside the pom.xml file as below.

```
<dependencies>

  <dependency>
    <groupId>junit</groupId>
    <artifactId>junit</artifactId>
    <version>4.11</version>
    <scope>test</scope>
  </dependency>
  <!-- https://mvnrepository.com/artifact/org.seleniumhq.selenium/selenium-java -->
  <dependency>
    <groupId>org.seleniumhq.selenium</groupId>
    <artifactId>selenium-java</artifactId>
    <version>4.1.3</version>
  </dependency>
  <!-- https://mvnrepository.com/artifact/io.github.bonigarcia/webdrivermanager -->
  <dependency>
    <groupId>io.github.bonigarcia</groupId>
    <artifactId>webdrivermanager</artifactId>
    <version>5.1.1</version>
  </dependency>
  <!-- https://mvnrepository.com/artifact/org.testng/testng -->
  <dependency>
    <groupId>org.testng</groupId>
    <artifactId>testng</artifactId>
    <version>7.5</version>
    <scope>test</scope>
  </dependency>

</dependencies>
```

And that's it. We are ready to write the Selenium program here and continue the page object model.

Maven project creation in Eclipse

Open eclipse

1. Click on file → new → project (not java project)

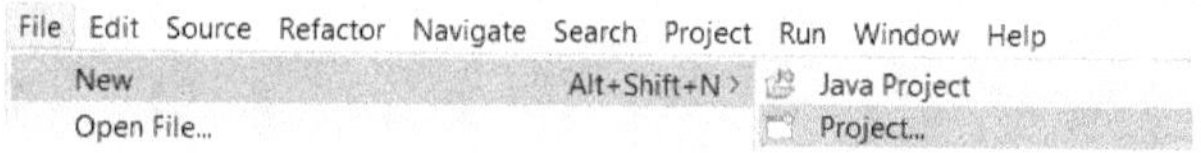

2. select maven project and next

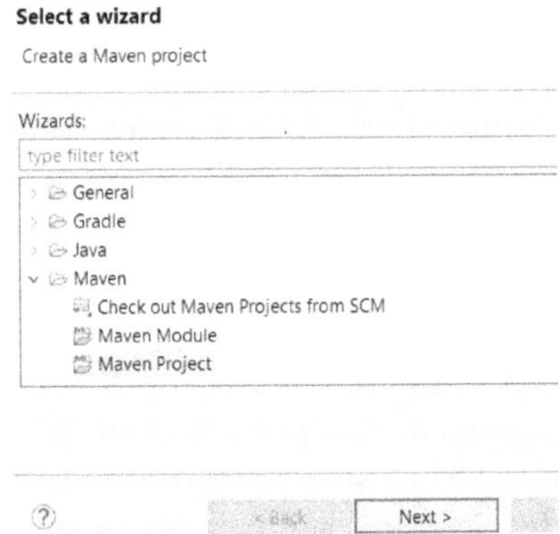

3. again next

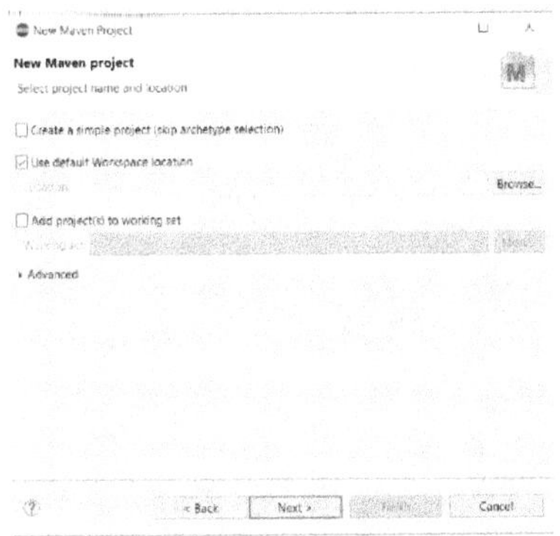

4. on next window wait till the archetypes gets pop upped
5. in the filter type → maven-archetype-quickstart
6. select 'maven-archetype-quickstart' from the org.apache.maven.archtypes

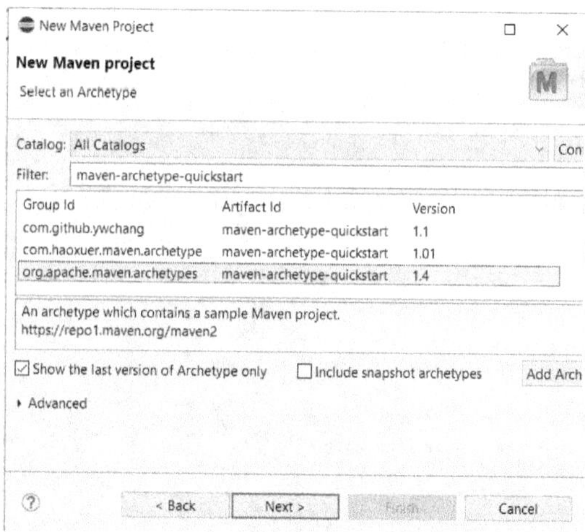

wait for some time, and it will create your maven project
Add the dependencies of selenium, testing, etc., as seen in IntelliJ ideas.

Object Repository :

Login Page :

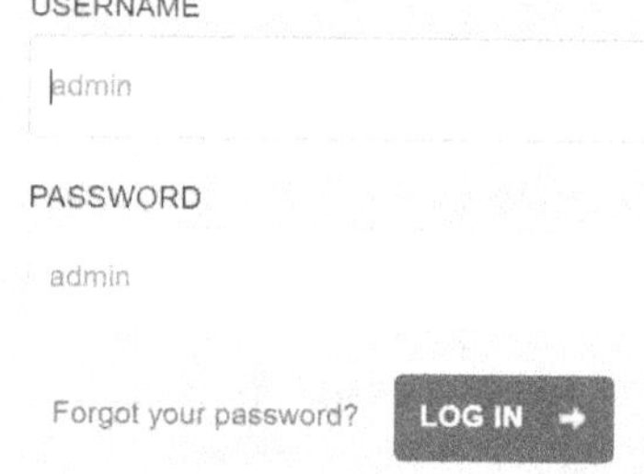

on this login page we can see there are below elements

1. Username label
2. username textbox
3. password label

4. password textbox
5. forgot password link
6. login button

All of these elements must be stored in the object repository, and as we have discussed, there will be one class for one page. I am going to create a package inside the main Java package. Let us name it 'pages,' I will maintain all the pages from this project, for example, the login page.

```
∨  src
   ∨  main
      ∨  java
         ∨  pages
            c  Login
```

In the login class, let's maintain all the above webelements.

Generally, we find the web element As below.
WebElement txtUsername=
driver.findElement(By.*xpath*("//input[@id='email']"));

But in this Framework, we will use the page factory, and we will define the web elements as below.

@FindBy (xpath="//input[@id='email']")
WebElement txtUsername;

Both the statements will generate the web element txtUsername similarly. Let's find the other elements as well below.

@FindBy (xpath="//input[@id='password']")
WebElement txtPassword;

```
@FindBy (xpath = "//button[normalize-space()='Login']")
WebElement btnLogin;
```

```
@FindBy(xpath = "//a[normalize-space()='I forgot my
password']")
WebElement lnkForgotPassword;
```

```
@FindBy (xpath="//label[@for='email']")
WebElement lblEmail;
```

```
@FindBy (xpath="//label[@for='password']")
WebElement lblPassword;
```

Now let's write operating methods are actions.

1. Action for txtUsername: this web element is a text box, so the operation or the action on this element will be sendKeys. Let's write a function for it.

```
public void setTxtUsername(String username)
{
  txtUsername.sendKeys(username);
}
```

This function will be called inside the test whenever we will have to interact with the user name text box.

2. Action for txtPassword: this web element is a text box, so the operation or the action on this element will be sendKeys. Let's write a function for it.

```java
public void setTxtPassword(String password)
{
  txtPassword.sendKeys(username);
}
```

3.   Action for btnLogin: this web element is a button, so the operation or the action on this element will be 'click'; below is its action method.

```java
public void clickLogin()
{
  btnLogin.click();
}
```

Similarly, you can also write the web elements like forgot password link and the levels. You can write the actions for them.

Let's write the test for this login page.

In the test section, we will add a LoginTest.java class.

```java
public class LoginTest {
  @Test
  public void loginTest() throws IOException {
//——------ code to open browser and URL–
WebDriverManager.chromedriver().setup();
driver – new ChromeDriver();
driver.manage().window().maximize();
driver.get("http://stock.scriptinglogic.net");

//——------ code to interact with the webpage–
```

```
Login login = new Login(driver);


    login.setTxtUsername("admin");
    login.setTxtPassword("admin");
    login.clickLogin();
  }



}
```

In the above code, you can see after we write the code to open the URL and the web page, I have created an object of the login class. Using this object, I call the methods to set the username and password, and lastly, I click the login button.

Forgot password Page :

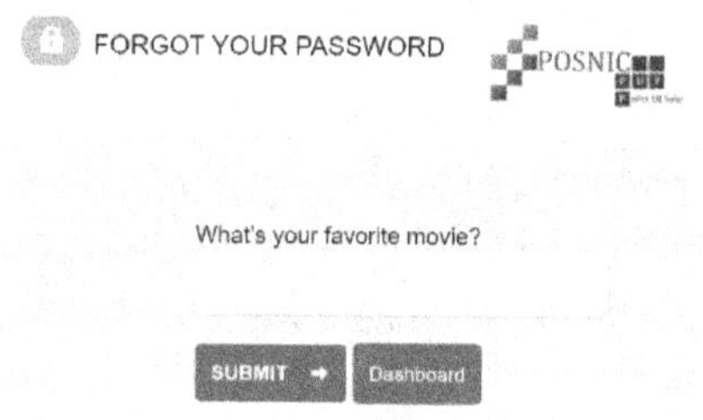

On this page we have below elements

'What's your favorite movie?' label

1. a text box
2. submit button
3. Dashboard button

Let's find these Web elements, and we will create a class ForgotPassword under the package pages.

```
v  main
   v  java
      v  pages
            C  ForgotPassword
            C  Login
```

@FindBy (xpath="//input[@id='name']")
WebElement textBox;

@FindBy (xpath = "//input[@name='submit']")
WebElement btnSubmit;

@FindBy(xpath = "//a[normalize-space()='Dashboard']")
WebElement btnDashboard;

Now let's write operating methods are actions.

1. Action for textBox: this web element is a text box, so the operation or the action on this element will be sendKeys. Let's write a function for it.


```java
public void setTextBox(String answer)
{
  textBox.sendKeys(answer);
}
```


This function will be called inside the test whenever we will have to interact with the user name text box.

2.   Action for btnSubmit: this web element is a button, so the operation or the action on this element will be 'click.' Below is its action method.

```
public void clickSubmit()
{
  btnSubmit.click();
}
```

let's write a test for this page
in the test section, we will add a ForgotPasswordTest.java class

```
v  test
  v  java
    v  regression
        ForgotPasswordTest
        LoginTest
```

public class ForgotPasswordTest {

@Test
public void forgotPasswordTest() throws IOException {


```
WebDriverManager.chromedriver().setup();
WebDriver driver = new ChromeDriver();
driver.manage().window().maximize();
driver.get("http://stock.scriptinglogic.net");
```


```
Login login = new Login(driver);
login.clickForgotPassword();
```


```
ForgotPassword forgotPassword = new ForgotPassword(driver);
```

```
    forgotPassword.setTexBox("xyz");
    forgotPassword.clickSubmit();
  }
}
```

Understand that when we open the URL, we don't get the forgot password page directly, but we have the forgot password link on the login page, so we create the object of the login class, and we call the method to click on the forgot password link. After that, we create the object of the forgot password class, type it into the textbox and click on the submit button.

Importance Properties File

We work in an organization with different environments for the projects. Environment means it is a platform where your project build is hosted. It is for the apparent reason that when the build is ready, we will not directly upload it to the production server. We might first upload it to your local server, then the pre-production server, and then to the production servers. So you have three total environments: local, pre-production, and production environments. We will upload the same build there. Whatever test scripts you will write will be the same for all of these environments. It's just that the URL might change, or the username or password might change. So in case your environment changes, you will have to change the URL in each class/test where you have used it. To avoid this, we maintain a properties file. We retain key-value pairs like URL, username, and password, read that properties file, and use those values of the key inside our test. So if your environment changes, we will change the properties file only and reflect the same in every test.

Let's see how to implement this. Below are the steps

```
1. read the file
FileInputStream fileInputStream = new
FileInputStream("Config/config.properties");
```

2. create the object of the properties class
Properties prop = new Properties();

3. load the file object with properties object
prop.load(fileInputStream);

4. read the value of the key using the loaded properties object

String myurl = prop.getProperty("url");

System.*out*.println("URL="+myurl);

Let's implement this in our project.
I will create one folder. I will call this folder a config
inside this, I will create a file with the name config.properties

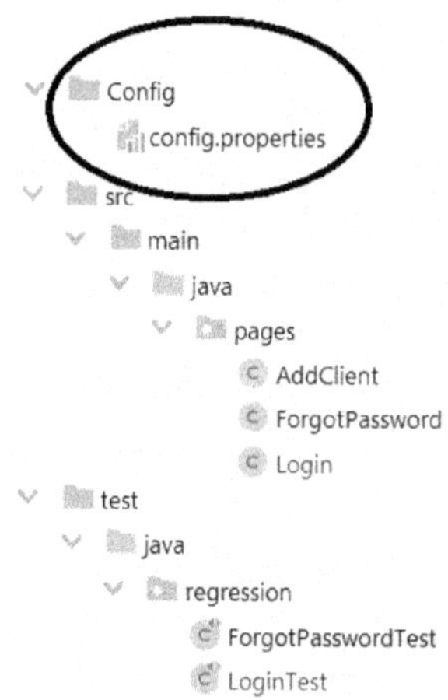

Note: when you will right click on a folder, you will not get any option to create a properties file to create a regular file with the extension dot properties

Now let's create a class under the new package utility of the main Java.

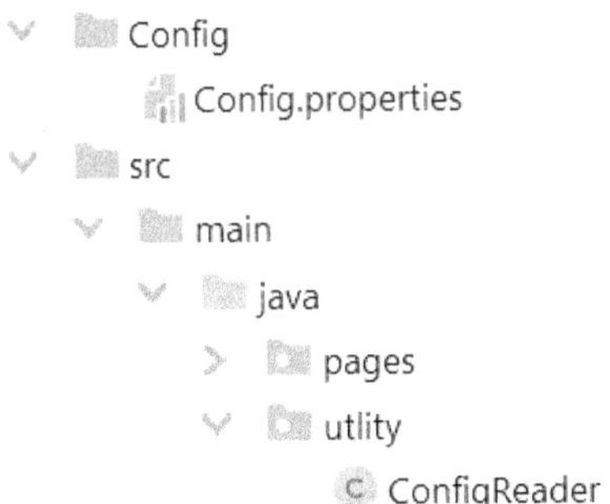

In this class, we will implement the code to read the value of the key from the properties file.

First, we will create a method to create the properties object loaded with the file object. The return type will be Properties.

```java
Properties getLoadedPropertiesObject() throws IOException {
    // 1. read the file
    FileInputStream fis = new
FileInputStream("Config/Config.properties");
    // 2. Create the object of the properties class
    Properties prop = new Properties();
    // 3 . load the file object with properties object
    prop.load(fis);


    return prop;
}
```

Now we will create individual methods that will return the value of a key.

```java
public static String getUrl() throws IOException {
  return getLoadedPropertiesObject().getProperty("url");
}
```

Understand here *getLoadedPropertiesObject()* method holds the loaded properties object. So we can directly use this method to call the getProperty() method, which will give us the value of the URL in the form of a string.

This method is static. So to call this method, we will not need to create the object of this class. as this method is static, we have learned that the static method does not allow non-static methods. So here *getLoadedPropertiesObject()* method also has to be made static as below.

```java
static Properties getLoadedPropertiesObject() throws IOException
{
    // 1. read the file
  FileInputStream fis = new
FileInputStream("Config/Config.properties");
    // 2. Create the object of the properties class
  Properties prop = new Properties();
    // 3 . load the file object with properties object
  prop.load(fis);


  return prop;
}
```

Similarly, you can get the other values as well below.

```java
public static String getUsername() throws IOException {
    return getLoadedPropertiesObject().getProperty("username");
}


public static String getPassword() throws IOException {
    return getLoadedPropertiesObject().getProperty("password");
}
```

Maven and Jenkins

Let's run the project on a command prompt using maven commands.

We have seen how to create a project in Maven. In real-time, to run this project, the better way is to run on a command prompt using some commands through Maven. To implement this, consider the below steps

- We should create a project in Maven
- Download maven: https://maven.apache.org/download.cgi
- Set path

c. go to system properties → environment variables. Create a variable MAVEN_HOME and paste the path of the maven folder

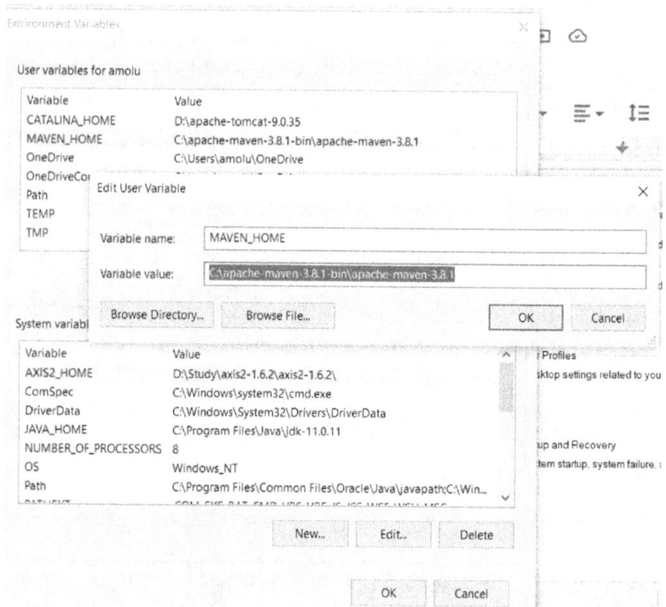

b. Go to the path variable and add the maven path till bin.

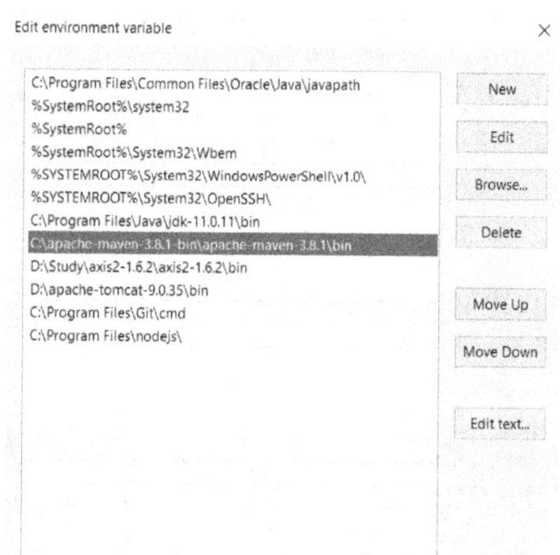

- Make sure that you have a sure-fire plugin in your pom.xml (you will have it if you are following the above steps to create a maven project, so don't worry)
- Open command prompt
- Go to your project path and type.

- mvn test
- All the java files in the test section will run.

if you have a testng.xml file in your project and you want to run that, then

- Add the below code to run your testing.xml (created at the project level) in your pom.xml

```
<plugin>
  <artifactId>maven-surefire-plugin</artifactId>
  <version>2.22.1</version>

  <configuration>
    <suiteXmlFiles>
      <suiteXmlFile>testng.xml</suiteXmlFile>
    </suiteXmlFiles>
  </configuration>

</plugin>
```

- (refer to this link https://maven.apache.org/surefire/maven-surefire-plugin/examples/testng.html)
- mvn test (same command)

Let's run the project on a command prompt using Jenkins.

Remember, the Jenkins will be already installed in your organization. So while working in the organization, you don't have to worry about the installation part. Since you have to practice it on your local machine, so to download and install the Jenkins use the below link https://www.jenkins.io/download/

you will get guidelines to install it on your device on the same website.
Login and continue

When you will log in the first time, go to the Global tool configuration from the manage Jenkins option

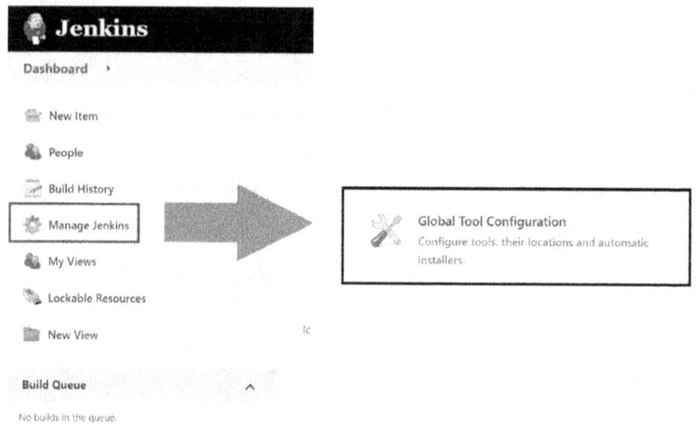

There set the JDK and the maven path.

Now go back to the dashboard, click on a new item, type the name of your project, select freestyle project, and say ok.

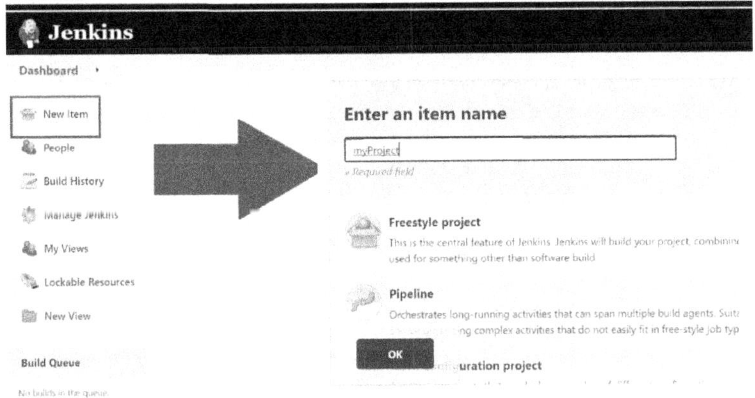

Go to the Jenkins workspace path, create a folder (use the same name as your item name in the recent step), and place your project there.

Generally, the Jenkins workspace will have a path like this on windows.

C:\ProgramData\Jenkins\.jenkins\workspace

Now go to the build, click on add build step, then select execute Windows batch command if you are working on Windows; otherwise, you can select execute shell, then you have to hit the two commands
CD folderName
mvn test

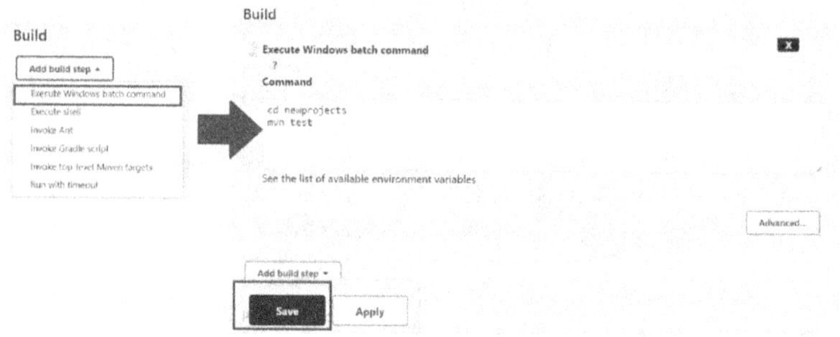

Now go to your project and click on build now.

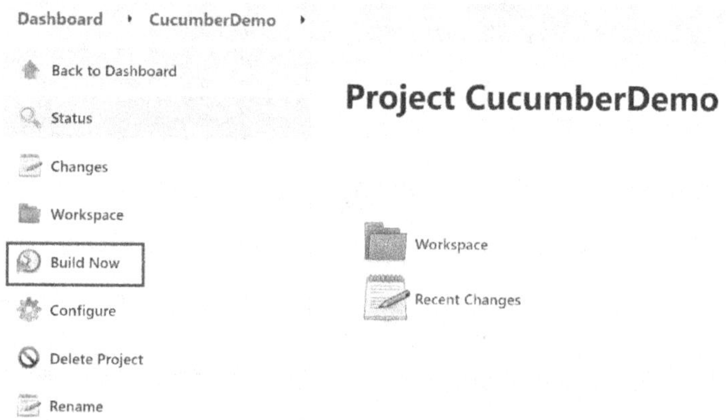

It will start executing your project. You can see its log-in console output below.

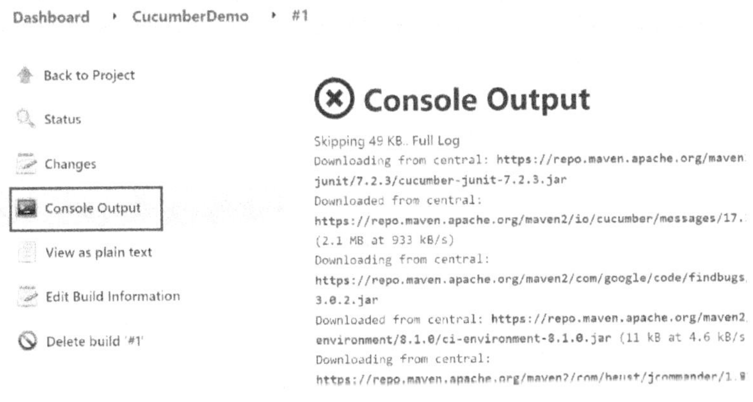

Thanksgiving

I want to thank you for reading this book. In case if you have any queries, you can stay in touch with me on my social network.

Do subscribe to my YouTube channel you are inevitably going to get lots of useful stuff that is going to help you to grow your career

http://youtube.com/amolujagare

My social links

http://facebook.com/amol.ujagare
https://www.linkedin.com/in/amolujagare
https://www.instagram.com/iamamolujagare

My websites and blogs

http://amolujagare.com
http://scriptinglogic.com
http://scriptinglogic.org

Lastly, I want to wish you best luck for your career.

Thank You

- Amol Ujagare